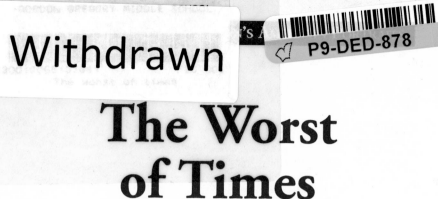

The Worst of Times

James Lincoln Collier

JAMESTOWN PUBLISHERS

a division of NTC/Contemporary Publishing Group
Lincolnwood, Illinois USA

For Colby

Cover Credits
   Design: Herman Adler Design Group
   Illustration: David Schweitzer
   Timeline: (left) David & Charles (Holding) Ltd.,
   London/William Morrow, New York;
   (middle) Franklin D. Roosevelt Library;
   (right) Everett Collection

ISBN: 0-8092-0579-3 (hardbound)
ISBN: 0-8092-0621-8 (softbound)

Published by Jamestown Publishers,
a division of NTC/Contemporary Publishing Group, Inc.,
4255 West Touhy Avenue,
Lincolnwood (Chicago), Illinois 60712-1975 U.S.A.

   01 02 03 04 ML 10 9 8 7 6 5 4 3 2

Chapter 1

On Saturday morning Mom sent me down to Santini's grocery store for eggs and a couple of other things. We were going over to Uncle Mort's at lunchtime to hear President Roosevelt's inaugural address, and Mom had told Aunt Mae that she would bring a cake. Not that she had to, for Uncle Mort and Aunt Mae had a cook and maids to serve us, and there would be plenty of food. But Mom always liked to bring something anyway.

I was coming out of the store holding the paper bag under one arm, when this kid came out of the dark alley alongside the store, where Mr. Santini kept his garbage cans. The kid was wearing the most raggedy clothes I ever saw on anybody. The toes of his shoes had split open and his own toes were sticking out, bare and dirty, because he had no socks. There were holes in both knees of his pants. His jacket was dirty and rumpled, like it hadn't been cleaned for months, and one pocket was ripped off and hanging down. Under the jacket he wore just a dirty brown sweater filled with holes. His black hair looked like it had been cut with a knife and stuck out in all directions. He was skinny and there were dark circles under his eyes. I judged he was about 12, my age. He was half-crouched, shoving something into his mouth. His eyes were wide, scared that he'd been caught at something.

He stared at me and I stared at him. He swallowed and took his hand away from his mouth. "I know you," he said. "You're Petey Williamson."

I was startled. "How come you know me?"

He took a quick look around as if he were getting ready to make a run for it. "I'm Charlie Henrich."

"You're Charlie Henrich?" I could hardly believe it.

He was still crouching, ready to run. "Nobody around here recognizes me anymore. Nobody wants to."

Suddenly he came into focus and I saw that it was him. How come I hadn't recognized him before? He used to live a couple of blocks away from us. We would walk home from school together. A lot of times I'd go over to his house to play. He had a lot of stuff to play with— boxing gloves and a punching bag, a microscope, a fancy set of Lionel trains with gondola cars that tipped when you pressed a button and a derrick car for unloading stuff. I spent a lot of afternoons with him. Then he was gone.

We always spent summers out at Gramps's farm—me, Mom, my older sister Ruth—because it wasn't supposed to be healthy for kids in the city in hot weather. Dad came out on weekends mostly. When I came back to Chicago one fall, Charlie wasn't there anymore. Somebody said the Henrichs had moved away, and Charlie drifted out of my mind.

The whole thing was giving me a mighty strange feeling. My past was changing while I stood there staring at it. "What happened to your clothes?" I blurted out. It

2

wasn't right to make fun of people's clothes, but I figured he knew I didn't mean any harm.

He looked down at his jacket and put his hand over the torn pocket to hold it together. "You wouldn't believe it if I told you, Petey."

"Yes, I would."

He stared into my face. "My dad killed himself."

I blinked. "He killed himself?" It was unbelievable: people killed themselves in books. Real people you knew didn't kill themselves.

"He couldn't stand everything that happened to him. He shouldn't have done it; me and Mom needed him. But he did. When the Depression hit, he went broke. He was vice-president of the Merchant's National Bank over there on Clark Street. A couple of months after the stock market crash in 1929 the bank folded up. They said Dad had done something wrong. It wasn't true, some other people laid the blame on him for what they did. But he couldn't prove it and he went to jail."

"Jail?" My mouth dropped open. That was unreal too. "Your dad went to jail?"

"He was in jail for a year. When he came out he couldn't get a job, any kind of a job. One day he went out to a pawnshop, bought a little pistol and shot himself in the head. The pistol was a cheap one, the bullets weren't any good, and he had to shoot himself twice before he was dead."

I was feeling stranger and stranger. It was like I'd gone to bed at home as usual and woke up in China. I wondered if Charlie had seen his Dad when he was lying there dead, but I didn't ask. "What did you do?"

"Me and Mom went to live with my Uncle Harry. Mom couldn't take the whole thing and spent half her time in bed crying."

"Why doesn't your uncle buy you some shoes?"

"I don't live there anymore. He had a furniture store on Kinzie Street. He kept it going for a while after the '29 crash, but then it went under. The whole thing got on Uncle Harry's nerves—no money, Mom crying, me another mouth to feed. He would blow up at me whenever anything went wrong, and if I tried to say it wasn't my fault he'd smack me. I hated getting smacked all the time, so I ran away. Stole $12 from his wallet when he was sleeping, put my clothes and as much food as I could in a paper bag, and left."

"Couldn't you go back?"

"I did. After three months I got tired of begging and being cold and went back. Uncle Harry didn't want me back, but Mom fell down on her knees and cried like a waterfall, and he gave in. But a week later he hit me so hard he knocked me clear across the room. He turned to walk away. I snatched up the poker from the fireplace and hit him over the head with it. Then I ran out of there for good. At the door I looked back. He was lying on the floor bleeding from the head, but he was breathing, so I figured I hadn't killed him. I'd do it again, too, if I had the chance."

Charlie had changed, that was for certain. Back when I used to play trains with him he'd been a sort of quiet kid, maybe a little shy. Now he was stealing money and hitting grownups on the head. If he'd been some kid from a different place I didn't know anything about, like Romania or Uruguay, it might have made sense, the way unbelievable stuff makes sense in books. But once he'd been a kid like me, with a mom and a dad and Lionel trains. "Where are you living now?" I asked him.

"In that Hooverville out behind the railroad yards."

"Hooverville?"

"You've never heard of a Hooverville, Petey?"

I felt embarrassed. "Maybe I have. I forget."

"It's a shacktown. Shantytown. They have lots of names for them. There's hundreds of people out there living in shacks. I got one of my own."

"What do you do for food?"

"What do you think I do for food, Petey?"

"I don't know."

"Beg. That's why I came over here to the north side. People have money over here. Sometimes you can swipe stuff over here."

"You steal? Aren't you afraid of being caught?"

"Naw," he said. "They're not going to put a kid as young as me in jail. All they'll do is whack you around a little and tell you to beat it."

It was funny—he was boasting about it, to show me how tough he was now. "Is that what you were doing in the alley—looking for something to steal?"

"It isn't stealing when you take it out of garbage cans. That's legal."

"You were eating stuff out of garbage cans?" It made me kind of sick to think about it.

"Over in shacktown nobody thinks anything about it. Sometimes you'll find half a cake or a big piece of fried chicken."

He was trying to act casual and tough about it. "Couldn't you get sick eating stuff like that?"

He shrugged. "Probably. What difference does it make? I feel lousy most of the time anyway." Suddenly he put his hands over his face and began to cry. "You don't know what it's like, Petey. None of you do. I just feel lousy all the time." He took his hands off his face to look at me. For a minute he couldn't say anything, but then he shook himself and stopped crying. "I'm sorry," he said. "I didn't mean to cry. Mostly I don't. But meeting up with you brought it all back." He wiped his eyes with the sleeve of his dirty jacket. "Petey, I haven't had anything to eat since yesterday morning. I found a doughnut with a bite out of it in that garbage can. That's what I was eating when I saw you."

I couldn't think of anything to say. Charlie might as well have been telling me about what it was like to live in China—not someplace I could get to on a streetcar. I reached my hand in my pocket and pulled out the change from the dollar Mom had given me. A quarter and three pennies. I held them out to him. "It's all I've got," I said. "I've got to go. Mom's waiting for the eggs and things."

He snatched the change out of my palm. "Thanks, Petey. Thanks a lot. For a quarter I can get a fried-egg sandwich, custard pie, and coffee." He looked kind of ashamed of himself for begging from an old friend, but he was too hungry to care.

"Maybe I'll come over and visit you," I said.

"Oh yes," he said. "Please come, Petey. You'll see for yourself."

I looked at my watch. It was real late. "I've got to go. Maybe I'll see you."

Chapter 2

Meeting Charlie Henrich like that bothered me in a lot of ways, but the way it bothered me most was that I'd never had any idea how bad the Depression was. Of course you saw pictures of people on strike in the newspapers, and heard about stocks and bonds going down on the radio, but I'd never paid much attention to it. It was just newspaper stuff. The only part of the newspaper I ever read was the sports—I was a big Cubs fan. The Cubs had won the pennant in '32, but they'd got licked by the Yankees 4–1 in the series, and we were all hoping to get revenge. But now, suddenly, I realized that it wasn't just newspaper stuff. How come I hadn't known before?

I remembered: Sometimes, when we were driving out to Gramps's farm, we'd see a family with little packs on their shoulders walking along the road. Just trudging along, not talking—a mom, a dad, two or three kids of different sizes, maybe the Mom carrying a baby. They'd be dressed real shabby, the kids likely to have holes in the seats of their pants, and their knees, too. According to Dad, all they owned they were carrying on their backs.

"Where are they going?"

Dad would shrug. "I guess they don't know where they're going. Looking for work, any kind of work. They hope they'll find a farmer who needs a hired man out here."

I would look out the rear window, watching them get smaller and smaller down the road. "What's going to happen to them?"

"I don't know, Petey. There's millions like that now. Let's hope they find something."

So I should have known, but I hadn't. They were just people I saw through a car window, getting smaller down the road.

I came to our house. I'd never thought about it before. It was just our house. I'd lived there since I was born. It wasn't new—built in 1906, so it was over 25 years old. Stucco on the outside, little front porch with a glider where you could sit on hot summer nights, a room for my sister Ruth who was away at Aurora College, a room for me. We had an electric icebox, an Oriental carpet in the living room, a phonograph, and a piano so Ruth could have lessons. "It isn't a palace," Dad would say, "but it isn't bad for a kid who grew up on a farm." Dad had done real well for himself and he was proud of it.

But so had Charlie's dad; and now Charlie was living in a shack and eating out of garbage cans.

Mom was in the kitchen, sifting flour into her big yellow bowl with the blue stripe around it. "What took you so long? I've got to get the cake in the oven."

"Something funny happened. I ran into this kid I used

to know. Charlie Henrich. You remember him, Mom?"

She gave me a quick glance. "Yes, I remember. You always wanted Lionel trains like his, but Dad said there was a limit. Where are the eggs?"

I put the bag down on the table and took out the eggs. "He's poor now. He lives in some shacktown. He hasn't got any socks and his shoes are all ripped up."

She shook her head. "The poor kid. I thought they'd gone to live with his uncle."

I was having a lot of surprises. "You knew about that?"

She looked at me. "Yes. I can't say we knew the Henrichs particularly, but I'd see Charlie's mother at PTA meetings."

I stared at her. "Did you know Charlie's dad killed himself? He had to shoot himself twice before he was dead?"

She didn't say anything for a minute, but began cracking eggs and dropping the yolks into the big yellow bowl. Then she said, "Yes, we knew."

"How come you never told me?"

She didn't say anything for a minute, but went on cracking eggs. Then she said, "At first we thought you must know—that the kids at school would have been full of it. But when you never said anything about it we realized that word hadn't gotten around school. We decided not to tell you."

"Mom, you should have told me. That wasn't right. He was my friend, not yours."

"I know, Petey. We didn't want to trouble you with it.

There are enough things to worry about these days. We thought it might give you nightmares."

"So what if I had nightmares? You should have told me. Look at Charlie, living in a shack and eating garbage. That's a lot worse than a nightmare."

She looked at me over her glasses the way she did. "How much did you give him?"

I flushed. But I would have had to tell her anyway. "The change from the dollar. It was 28 cents. I'll pay you back."

She poured the cake batter into the cake pan and slid it into the oven. Then she straightened up and looked at me. "Petey, I don't mind about the money. I can spare 28 cents. But you have to realize that Charlie Henrich isn't the only poor kid around. We can't feed them all out of my food budget." She stared at me a minute more, thinking. Then she said, "Petey, things are a little tight for us, too, right now." She clapped her hands. "Now go wash up and change your clothes. I've put out your good pants and a clean shirt."

Dad got home just before noon. I put on my topcoat, for it was March, still cold. We got into the Buick and drove over to Uncle Mort's house. Uncle Mort was Mom's brother. Dad had done well for himself, but Uncle Mort had done real well. They had a big stone house that was supposed to look like a miniature castle out of a King Arthur book—slate roof with four chimneys, a turret to one side where Uncle Mort and Aunt Mae slept, windows with arches over them.

Uncle Mort owned his own company called Rayfield Chrome. They chromium-plated parts for automobiles—gas caps, hubcaps, radiator ornaments. You wouldn't think you could get rich off stuff like that, but you could. Uncle Mort had three cars—a Ford station wagon for Aunt Mae, a Packard he drove to work every day, and a Cadillac for special occasions. They had a cook, two maids, and a yard man who put on a uniform and chauffeured them when they went out in the Caddy. Uncle Mort even looked rich—fat, with a big mustache and his vest pulled tight across his tummy.

We went in to lunch right away, so as not to miss Roosevelt's inaugural speech. Cousin Steve was there, Aunt Helen with the little cousins, us, an old friend of Aunt Mae's, a dozen people, maybe, all hoping that President Roosevelt would have some ideas for bringing back good times.

I hoped I could sit by Steve. He was my friend, even though he was seven years older than me, and going to the University of Chicago. He didn't look down on me the way most college guys would look down on a kid in seventh grade. He always talked to me like I was his age. He used to read to me when I was younger. Mom read me *Winnie-the-Pooh* and stuff, but Steve read to me out of his pulp magazines—*Short Story, Ace High*. War stories, or guys trapped in submarines.

Steve was studying political science at the university. Uncle Mort said it was a lot of bunk cooked up by professors with their heads in the clouds. He wanted Steve to study something realistic, like engineering. But Steve was more interested in philosophy and stuff like that. He was tall, skinny, a lot of blond hair, got straight A's, played clarinet in the football band, was on the tennis team, always had some pretty girl with him. It made me proud to have somebody like Steve for a friend.

So I wished he'd come and sit next to me, but he was across the room talking to Aunt Helen, and they put me between the little cousins so they couldn't hit each other.

There wasn't any shortage of food. Mom always said that was one thing about Aunt Mae, she didn't stint. White tablecloth, crystal glasses, silverware that Mom said cost hundreds of dollars. A huge bowl of potato salad, a platter of cold corned beef, another platter of cold chicken, a hot pot of macaroni and cheese, a bowl of pickled beets, three kinds of relishes, dill pickles, iced tea for the grownups, milk for us kids. There'd be Mom's cake afterwards, and I was pretty sure there'd be pie and ice cream too. I wondered: was Charlie Henrich eating his fried-egg sandwich right then? Hungry as he'd been, I figured he'd run for the lunch counter as soon as I'd turned my back.

Uncle Mort had the groundsman carry the big Stromberg-Carlson radio into the dining room so we could hear the speech while we ate our cake, pie and ice cream—like I figured, Aunt Mae wouldn't rest content with Mom's cake. I wasn't much for speeches, but I listened to this one pretty carefully. Partly that was so I wouldn't look foolish if Steve started talking to me about it, which he was likely to do. But mostly it was because I'd suddenly woke up to a lot of things. Maybe Mom was right; maybe it would have given me nightmares to have known about Charlie's dad having to shoot himself in the head twice to kill himself. They should have told me, anyway. I wasn't going to let that happen anymore: I was going to find out for myself.

The speech went on for a while. The President said that the only thing we had to fear was fear itself, which I didn't quite get, but I got most of the speech. He had a plan to put young men without jobs to work in the countryside planting trees. He had another plan to keep farmers from having their farms foreclosed by the banks. I could see where that was important. I loved it out on Gramps's farm. The house was filled with old smells—wood smoke, kerosene, flowers, I don't know what. Gramps loved the farm too. He'd been born there, spent his life there. His younger brother, my uncle Jim Williamson, moved to California, but Gramps would never leave. Out front a tire swing hung from a branch of a big maple. Way at the back of the cow pasture was a creek where me and Ruth swam on hot days. There were some rocks along the bank, which would be hot from the sun, and we'd lie on them to get warm. There were blueberry bushes along the creek, and if we brought home a shirtful Grandma would make blueberry muffins for breakfast. Mom said we shouldn't collect blueberries in our shirts, for it stained them, but Grandma would laugh and say she'd been washing Gramps's overalls for forty years, she could get stains out of anything.

Across the front of the house was a veranda with a swinging bench Gramps had made, which hung from big hooks in the ceiling. I'd sit there sometimes after supper listening to the peepers and wait for the moon to suddenly rise up out of the cornfield like a huge pumpkin, turning the cornstalks to black and silver, until Mom made me go to bed. After she tucked me in and turned off the light I'd wait until I heard her footsteps going down the stairs and then I'd get up and lean out the window to look at the moon some more.

Then there was applause coming through the radio. Uncle Mort leaned over and turned it off. Nobody said anything for a minute. Then Uncle Mort said, "I don't trust him. He's too slick for me. It sounds like he wants to hand out government jobs to millions of people to get their votes." He bent over his dish and took a big spoonful of cherry ice cream. "How's he going to pay for it? He'll want to raise taxes, that's for sure." He sat up straight and looked around the table to see if anyone wanted to argue with him. Mostly people didn't argue with Uncle Mort.

Then Dad said, "I think we have to give him a chance, Mort. The other fellows weren't able to solve anything. I don't like giving people handouts, either. Who's going to work if they can get a government check? But this idea of putting people to work planting trees, something useful like that, might do some good."

"It's a smoke screen, Uncle Vic," Steve said to Dad.

"Roosevelt isn't going to change anything basic. He should be taking over the banks, have the government run them for the general good, not for private profit."

Uncle Mort stared at Steve. "What's so bad about private profit, son?"

Dad took a quick look at Uncle Mort, who was beginning to grow red. Then he turned back to Steve. "Look, Steve, we're all willing to grant that some of the banks, the Wall Street stockbrokers, the money people, were out of bounds. We read the newspapers. And some of them are going to jail for what they did back in the '20s when everybody thought good times would never end. I agree that the government ought to have kept a closer eye on the banks, especially, so's they wouldn't go under the way so many have. But the capitalist system is what's made this nation so prosperous, and it depends on private profit. Why would anybody go to the trouble of starting a business, creating all those jobs, if he couldn't make a profit out of it? Your dad's a perfect example. Look at the jobs he's created. He deserves to make a profit."

I took a quick glance at Uncle Mort. He'd calmed himself down some and was listening carefully, turning his head to each person. "What prosperity is that you're talking about, Uncle Vic?" Steve said. "You've got 10 million people out of work, Negroes in the South living in shacks you wouldn't put a dog into, farmers losing their homes."

Now Uncle Mort raised his hand, and we all turned to

look at him. "Steve," he said, not bursting out the way he usually did, but speaking quietly. "I notice you've never minded taking the profits of the capitalistic system for yourself. Private schools, your own car, servants at home, a college education. What right have you to bite the hand that feeds you?"

There was a silence, and everybody turned to look at Steve. He leaned forward, one elbow on the table, the other hand slowly spinning a knife round and round on the white tablecloth. For a minute he sat there saying nothing, looking down at the spinning knife, thinking out what he meant to say. Finally he looked up and began, speaking softly. "You know, Pop, I've been thinking the very same thing for a while now. I can't go around complaining about capitalism and take your money at the same time. There are fellows at the university who do that, and it doesn't bother them. They say the system is crooked, and you should take anything out of it you can get. But I can't do it." He paused, picked up the knife he'd been spinning on the tablecloth, and waved it at the plates of pie, cake, bowls of melting ice cream. "We went through enough food at lunch to feed a poor family for a week. How can we justify it?" He looked around at us. "Maybe you all can. I can't." He paused again and took a deep breath. "I've decided to quit college to see if I can't find something useful to do for people. I can't go on playing tennis and arguing about political theory when people, millions of them, are going to bed hungry every night."

"Oh Steve," Aunt Mae cried, with almost a sob in her voice. "You can't leave college."

Uncle Mort raised his hand like a traffic cop. "Let him, Mae. Let him try it. He's been coddled all his life. We grew up hard, you and me and Victor. We know what it's like to put in ten, twelve hours a day, six days a week of hard labor." He looked at Dad. "More than that down on the farm, right Victor? We know what it's like to have coffee and bread for breakfast, beans and bread for supper. We're all glad we can live better than that now. Let Steve see what it's like out there. Let him go live in hobo camps, cook slum-gullion in a tin can over a fire by the railroad tracks, sleep on gravel wrapped up in a piece of canvas. He'll find out that a lot of these people his heart bleeds for aren't all the sweethearts he thinks they are. Let him find out that a little capitalistic pie and ice cream isn't so bad after all."

Chapter 3

"Dad, do you think Steve will really quit college?" We were driving home in the Buick, Dad and Mom in the front seat, me in the back. It was starting to rain, but Dad hadn't turned on the windshield wipers yet. He always said you have to wait until the windshield is really wet before you turn them on or the wipers just smear the dirt around.

Dad turned his head back to look at me. "I don't know, Petey."

There were a lot of things I wanted to know about. "Do you think he ought to?"

Dad drove along through the streets of Chicago, thinking about it. There weren't many people on the sidewalks because of the rain. "I'll say this, Petey: Your Uncle Morton's right when he says Steve's been coddled. Always had the best of everything. Been to Europe twice before he was 14, always had maids to pick up his room. By the time Mort was 14, he was working in a brewery corking bottles. I don't think Steve has any idea of what Uncle Mort went through getting his company going. Working 14 hours a day, running from bank to bank trying to find money so his people would get their pay envelopes on Saturday. It won't do Steve any harm to find out how things are out in the real world."

"If Steve's supposed to find out about the real world, how come you and Mom didn't want me to know about Charlie Henrich?"

He glanced around at me again. "How'd you find out about that?"

"He ran into the Henrich boy this morning, Victor," Mom said.

"His dad shot himself in the head twice. You should have told me about it."

"We thought it might give you bad dreams," Dad said. "You were only eight, remember."

"Maybe I could have helped him."

"I don't see what you could have done, Petey," Mom said.

"Maybe I could have gone to see him. Maybe he would have liked to have a friend."

They didn't say anything.

"You should have told me. You should have told me a lot of things. I never knew how bad things were for a lot of people. I heard about the Depression and all, but it didn't mean anything to me. It never seemed to bother any of us."

"Petey, you were eight years old when the stock market crashed," Dad said. "Why should a little kid have to worry about stuff like that?"

"I'm not eight anymore," I said.

"Petey gave the boy some change," Mom said.

"It wasn't much," I said. "Twenty-eight cents. Charlie

20

hadn't had anything to eat since yesterday. He said he could get a fried egg sandwich and pie for that. I wished I could have brought him over to Uncle Mort's today and let him fill himself up."

"Do you really think he hadn't had anything to eat or was just saying that to get your sympathy?" Dad said.

"Dad, he looked terrible. Thin, his shoes split, holes in his sweater."

Dad nodded. "Well, I suppose you were right to give him the money."

"I've got to help him some more," I said. "I can't let him go hungry like that."

"Petey," Mom said, "be realistic. You can't keep giving him money all the time."

I could see that. My allowance was a quarter a week. That wasn't going to go very far. "At least I could bring him some better clothes. I've got stuff in my closet I never wear."

"For one thing," Mom said sharply, "you're not going out to Shacktown." She swung around, with her arms over the back seat to look me in the face. "Under no circumstances, Petey. Do you understand me? I mean it. It was kind of you to give that boy the money. I know how you must have felt. I might have done the same. But you are absolutely not to go to that place."

"Why not? What's wrong with going there?" I was beginning to feel stubborn. Didn't I have any rights?

"Petey, Mom's right," Dad said. "It's too dangerous. A lot of the people in these Hoovervilles are just down on their luck and wouldn't do you any harm. But there's a lot

21

of riffraff there too. They see a nice, well-dressed kid, they'll knock you down, take your jacket or your shoes to sell for a couple of bucks."

"Dad, nobody would do that."

He shook his head. "Petey, I'm not exaggerating. You're like Steve, you've always been protected. You don't know how bad life is for a lot of people. They're desperate out there. They'll get into a fight over half a sandwich. The cops are always going out there to pick up somebody who got his head bashed over nothing. I don't want you to go out there."

I knew I was going to go out there. I wanted to see for myself. "Well, if I've been coddled like Steve, maybe I ought to see what it's like."

Once more he took his eyes off the road to turn around and look at me. "No. That's final. Do you hear me?"

I didn't say anything.

Mom turned around too. "Petey, did you hear your father?"

"Yes," I said, feeling pushed around and sore. "I heard."

For a bit nobody said anything. Finally Dad said, "Petey, it's kind of you to want to help that boy. But you've got to remember, this isn't ordinary times. There are 10 million out of work. Think of it, 10 million. And most everybody else taking pay cuts, working part-time. The Depression's touched almost everybody in the country. We can't help them all." He paused and thought for a moment. "All right, Petey," he said. "You don't want

22

us to protect you. What if I told you that Gramps might lose the farm?"

My mouth opened up and I sat there, unable to believe it. "Lose the farm?" My farm, with the tire swing where I'd swung so often, the creek I'd swum in summer after summer, the little room under the eaves where I'd leaned out the window and watched the moon rise into the sky? "He can't," I said.

Dad shook his head. "He can. He's no different from a million other farmers who've lost their homes. When times were good he borrowed money to buy that piece of land out beyond the creek. Now the price of milk is down so low he can hardly get along himself, much less pay back the loan. If he can't pay up, the bank will take the farm."

"Can't we help him, Dad?"

"We have," Mom said. "We lent him a thousand dollars. We haven't got anything else to give him."

"What about Uncle Jim? He's Gramps's brother. I thought he had a lot of money."

"He did, before the Depression. He hasn't got much now."

I hated even thinking about some other kid swinging on my tire swing, swimming in my creek. "Doesn't President Roosevelt have some plan for saving people's farms?"

"Well he said so. Said he was going to raise farm prices and stop these foreclosures. But it'll take a while, and it might not go through anyway. It'll be too late for Gramps."

I couldn't bear the thought of it. "Isn't there something we can do?"

"We've thought of everything," Dad said. We were quiet. Then he said, "Petey, since we've told you this much, you might as well know the rest. We're pretty close to the edge ourselves. I've had to take two pay cuts over the past three years, and it looks like I might have to take another one."

It took a couple of seconds for that to sink in. "You might lose your job like Mr. Henrich?"

"No, Petey. I won't lose my job. You don't have to worry about that. Mr. O'Connor knows I've always been loyal to the company. He won't fire me. He's said as much. But things are likely to be tight for a while. We make farm machinery, remember. Farmers in debt to banks aren't buying new threshers and hayrakes. We're running at less than 50 percent of capacity, and if things don't pick up in a couple of months we'll be laying off another 10 men. Our hope is to hang on and see if Roosevelt can get the farmers back on their feet. But if it doesn't come pretty soon it'll be too late for us. That's why we can't do anything more for Gramps."

I sat there staring out the window. I'd wanted to know, and now I did. It wasn't just Charlie Henrich, it was all of us. Of course Charlie was a lot worse off than I was, but still. How come I hadn't figured any of it out for myself? I'd seen about the Dust Bowl in the newsreels: all those farmers tying their stuff onto their cars, chairs and tables up on the roof, and driving off to California with a carload of kids. I knew what kind of business Dad was in—I'd been out to his plant often enough and seen those shiny hayrakes and balers lined up in rows on the blacktop. How come I hadn't figured it out for myself? It had all just been newsreel stuff to me, nothing to do with real people. I sat there staring out between Mom's and Dad's heads through the windshield onto the street. Dad still hadn't turned the wipers on, and the people on the sidewalk with their umbrellas were smudges of color, the neon signs snaky zigzags. "Did you tell Ruth?" I asked.

"We told her when she was home for Christmas," Mom said. "We had to let her know that she might not be able to go back to college in the fall. She might have to get a job to help out until times get better."

"Oh," I said. I remembered: One night after Christmas, Ruth had come upstairs crying. I was in bed and supposed to be asleep, but I was reading. When I asked her about it in the morning she wouldn't tell me why she'd been crying. Mom and Dad had told her not to tell me.

I sat there watching the colored snakes dance in the windshield, feeling strange. The world I lived in had suddenly changed—the moon turned purple, statues walking around, cats and dogs talking. It was like I'd been dreaming all my life and had finally woke up. I'd been living inside one of those glass balls where there's a little white church and a red barn, all as quiet and peaceful as could be. But outside it was different—the wind blowing a freezing rain into your face, water coming in through holes in your shoes. I'd been inside that glass ball for a long time, but now I was coming out into that freezing rain.

Chapter 4

Steve didn't live at home, he lived at the University of Chicago—he wanted to be able to come and go as he liked, he told me, and if he lived at home Aunt Mae would always want to know where he was going. But he came home to see his folks on Sundays sometimes, and the next Sunday I called him up, and he said he would drop around to see me on the way back to the university. He had a '31 Oldsmobile his dad had given him when he went to college to encourage him to come home fairly often. We got a couple of gloves and a ball, went out to the back lawn by the garage and tossed the ball around while we talked.

"Are you really going to quit the university, Steve?"

"Yes," he said. "I talked with my folks about it this morning. Pop said he'd already paid my tuition for the rest of the year and I owed it to him to finish the semester. But in June I'm gone."

"To where?"

"California, probably. There's a lot going on out there." He tossed me an easy, looping one. "They're trying to organize the fruit pickers, the longshoremen are ready to strike. Things are going to pop out there."

I tossed the ball back. "What would you do?"

"I don't know exactly. I'd like to get involved with the unions. That's where the action's going to be." He tossed me his big roundhouse curve. "I want to be in on it."

"That curve must have broken a foot," I said.

"Yeah," he said. "A curve like that looks good, but any good hitter'll murder it. I wouldn't try to get away with it in a game."

I tossed the ball back. "Why do you have to go all the way out to California? There are unions in Chicago."

"Sure, but what's going on in those migrant labor camps out there—fruit pickers, vegetable pickers—that's about the worst I've heard. You know, they get tractored off their farms in the Dust Bowl and go west looking for work. They've got whole families living in tents, washing their clothes in ditches."

I knew about the Dust Bowl out in Oklahoma, Arkansas, and Nebraska, where there'd been hardly any rain for years. "What do you mean, tractored off?"

"Because of the drought they can't grow much, and what they grow they can't get a decent price for. The banks foreclose, pull down their houses with tractors to open up more land."

"That may happen to Gramps," I said. Every time I thought of it I got an awful feeling, like I was going to have a hand chopped off or something.

"Your dad told me last weekend."

"They were keeping it from me. They've been keeping a lot of stuff from me. I'm pretty sore about it."

"They didn't want you to worry, Petey."

27

"Maybe it's up to me to decide if I should worry. What did they think, I'd never find out?"

"It's going to be terrible for Gramps. It's been terrible for a lot of people. All those Okies from the Dust Bowl loading up their families in old Model T Fords and heading west for the Promised Land. They end up living in tents and working 10 hours a day for 25 cents an hour. The whole family works, down to kids as young as six. They've got a perfect setup for a strike. The growers have to get the crop in when it's ripe—can't put it off. Of course they'll bring in scab labor."

I tried a curve, but it didn't break much. "What's a scab?"

"Really, Petey, you've got to start reading something besides the sports. Scabs are substitute workers. Plenty of people are so desperate for work they'll take any job for any wage, even if it means crossing a picket line and breaking a strike. Scabs, they call them. Or finks."

"Is that legal?"

"Sure it is. It's the grower's farm, he can hire anybody he wants. There's where the trouble comes in. Sometimes the strikers try to drive the scabs away. Stone them, go after them with baseball bats. People get hurt. The growers turn around and call in the sheriffs, and now you've got shotguns involved. People have been killed in these things." He held the ball up so I could see his fingers. "See where I've got them across the seams?" He threw the roundhouse again. "It's all legal," he continued. "Morally, that's another question. Why should a man have to put a six-year-old kid in the fields so he can earn enough money to live in a tent and wash his clothes in a ditch?"

"Maybe they should change the laws." I gripped the ball the way Steve had showed me and tried the curve. It broke a little better.

"There's a senator from New York, Robert Wagner, who wants to do that. Give the strikers some kind of rights so they've got a chance against the growers. Minimum-wage laws, child-labor laws, so they can't hire kids under a certain age, the way they do in the fields and the cotton mills. I think Roosevelt's going to support a lot of this stuff, but it's hard to tell with him."

He threw the ball back and I tried the curve again. "That's better," he said.

Finally I got around to what I wanted to talk to him about. "Steve, I ran into this kid I used to know when I was in second and third grade. Charlie Henrich, his name is. He's living in that shacktown over by the railroad yards. He used to live in a big house, had a great set of Lionel trains, all that stuff. Now he's living in a shack and wearing shoes that are split open in the front. I want to bring him some stuff, but Mom and Dad won't let me. They say it's dangerous to go over there."

Steve stood there, chucking the ball into his glove and thinking. "I don't know," he said finally. "They're bound to be cautious. Of course there are some pretty unpleasant characters in places like that. But mostly they're ordinary people who ran into trouble."

"You think I ought to go?"

"It isn't my business to tell you to disobey your parents."

"You're not much help," I said.

"What did you think I was going to say?"

"I suppose," I said. "I think I'm going to do it anyway."

"Let me put it this way," he said. "If you do, I'd like to hear about it."

I didn't disobey Dad and Mom very often. I don't know why, I just didn't. I guess it was because they didn't generally give me a lot of orders the way some kids' parents did. Eddie Driscoll wouldn't have been able to do anything at all if he hadn't disobeyed his parents a lot. Mostly what Dad and Mom told me made sense. But this time it didn't. If they'd told me about Charlie Henrich's father and all that when it happened, maybe I'd have been able to help him. Maybe if he'd had a friend, somebody to talk to and do things with, he might not have lost his temper with his uncle. Maybe he could even have come to live with us, or something. Maybe he still could. So it wasn't right for them to tell me I couldn't go over to the shacktown to see Charlie—not if I could help him some way.

On Saturday morning I put on my old corduroy knee pants, a flannel shirt, and my sneakers, for I had sense enough to know that I shouldn't go out to shacktown all dressed up. I took a pair of old socks out of my drawer and stuffed them under my windbreaker. I told Mom I was going to play baseball, and off I went.

30

I didn't know how long it would take to get there. I
looked at the Elgin watch that Gramps had given me one
year for Christmas. Ten after nine. I'd worked out the
route from a map. I set off down Bush Street, then
zigzagged down some side streets. Pretty soon I was out of
the north side and into a neighborhood of tenements—
garbage cans on the streets, old cars with rusty roofs,
dented fenders, missing hubcaps along the curb. Kids
were playing stickball, and when a breeze rose newspapers
rattled along the sidewalks. Here men in overcoats leaned
against building walls, two or three of them in a row, not
saying much, just leaning there to kill time. After that I
went through a factory district, nothing but five- and six-
story brick buildings, the bricks more black than red with
soot and dirt. But the factories were dead inside, no
lights, lots of broken windows, heavy chains and padlocks
on the doors. I kept on going, turned a corner, and
suddenly there it was, a flat stretch of ground covered
with a jumble of shacks and huts every which way. They
were made of leftovers, scraps of boards and planks, some
bare, some with peeling paint on them; windows from
out of henhouses and such, tin cans flattened out and
nailed on for roofing, old doors from buildings that had
been torn down, even tattered rugs hanging where a door
was supposed to be. Stovepipes stuck out of the roofs. A
few small, scrubby trees grew among the shacks and here
and there were clumps of brown weeds along the bottoms
of the shack walls. It was a place made of junk, ruined
stuff that had been thrown away.

Two or three places in the open spaces people had

gathered around oil drums with fires burning inside them—men, women, kids, babies held close to the heat by their mothers, old men with stubble on their chins, who shivered no matter how close to the fire they crept. Not a decent set of clothing on any of them: shabby overcoats, cloth caps, old fisherman's sweaters with holes all over, work boots, carpet slippers, the women dressed mostly in pants like the men. The people looked like they'd been thrown away, too, useless leftovers that weren't good enough to keep.

Suddenly I felt nervous. It was a pretty rough place all right. I could see what Dad had meant when he'd said they were desperate here. I'd have been desperate, too, if I'd lived like that. But I wasn't going to back down, no matter how nervous I felt.

How was I going to find Charlie? There were at least 50 shacks there, maybe more. Would I have to go from door to door asking at each one? Maybe some of the people standing around the fires would know. I felt the socks tucked under my windbreaker, to see if they showed. Then I walked over to the nearest group of people gathered around a fire—six or seven of them— some older, some younger, a couple of women with kids.

They watched me come up, just watched, not saying anything. When I was 10 feet away I stopped. "I'm looking for a kid named Charlie Henrich. Does anyone know where he lives?"

Nobody spoke. They went on staring at me for a minute, and then they turned away and began talking among themselves in low voices about a fight somebody had had the night before. "Listen," I said, "I have some stuff for him he asked me to bring. His name's Charlie Henrich."

A couple of them looked at me. I pulled the socks out from under my shirt. "These socks. I'm bringing them for him."

They looked away again and went on with their conversation. I shoved the socks back under my windbreaker and backed away. Now what? I looked around. I didn't think I was going to have any better luck with another bunch, but what else could I do? So I walked over to another oil drum. "I'm looking for a kid named Charlie Henrich. I have something he asked me to bring."

One or two of them turned to look at me, but they didn't even stop talking among themselves. I backed away again and looked around. In the distance I could see people at other barrels looking at me—take a quick look, and then look away. I was more nervous than ever. What if they suddenly all came charging at me? Then I realized that one of the people at a barrel farther off was Charlie. Relief washed over me, and I started trotting towards him. When I was close enough, I called his name. But he'd already seen me, and was coming towards me.

"Nobody would tell me where you were," I said.

"They could see you weren't from here. They don't trust anybody who isn't from here. They don't trust a lot of people who *are* from here, either."

"These clothes aren't so hot. They're my baseball clothes."

"It's not just your clothes. It's everything. Hair cut and combed, fingernails clean, not slouched down but standing up straight."

"Mom wouldn't have let me leave the house with dirty fingernails or my hair not combed."

"That's the whole point, isn't it? If you'd messed yourself up a little it might have helped, but they'd still have known from your clothes."

"What did they think I was gong to do to them?" I said.

Charlie shrugged. "Nothing in particular. They just don't like strangers wandering around." Then he noticed the watch Gramps had given me. "Better take the watch off. Stick it down in your underpants."

I realized that I shouldn't have worn the watch out there at all. Why hadn't I thought of that? I slipped it off, but I didn't like the idea of walking around with it in my underpants, so I put it in my pants pocket.

"You ought to put it in your underpants," Charlie said.

"It'll be all right in my pocket," I said. "Nobody can see it there."

"If it was mine I'd put it in my underpants," he said.

"It'll be all right. Charlie, which one is your shack?"

"Over there. Come on, I'll show you." As we walked toward it, the thrown-away people kept giving me looks. I figured they wouldn't bother me so long as I was with

Charlie, but even so, I knew that they didn't want me around.

Charlie stopped in front of a shack that wasn't much different from the rest. "This is mine."

It had an old Oriental carpet tacked up for a door, and one small window frame nailed to the boards on the wall opposite the door. Most of the boards were gray, but a few of them had paint on them from whatever they'd originally been part of. "Can I look inside?"

He shrugged. "Go ahead if you want. There isn't much to see."

I stuck my head around the carpet. He was right, there wasn't much to see. A coal stove made out of a one-gallon lard can with holes punched around the bottom for a draft, a chair with the cane seat half ripped out, a mattress on the floor where he slept, with a couple of brown army blankets heaped up on it. On a little shelf over the bed sat a white mug, a tin plate, a knife and fork. Pinned to the walls with thumbtacks were a few pictures torn out of old calendars—an easy way to get pictures, for people threw away their calendars every year. One showed a white church in a village green, another a woman in a bathing suit, another a couple of monkeys wearing dresses and carrying parasols. There was also a picture of Gabby Hartnet, the Cubs catcher, wearing his chest protector, crouched down with his big catcher's glove in front of him. The place smelled old and musty, like wet wool.

I pulled my head out. It must be awful discouraging to come home to a place like that. Up on the north side some kids had better playhouses than Charlie's shack. No wonder he didn't make his bed. What was the point of it? But I supposed you got used to it. "Where do you go to the bathroom?" I asked.

He pointed over his shoulder with his thumb. "The city came in awhile back and put in some toilets. That's the only thing they've done for us."

I was glad I'd brought the socks to show him that at least somebody would do something for him. I reached under my windbreaker and took out the socks. "Here," I said. "I brought you these. It's all I could get away with. I'll try to bring you some more stuff later."

He looked at me. "You didn't have to bring me anything, Petey."

"I wanted to."

He snatched the socks out of my hand, sat right down on the ground and put them on. "There," he said, standing up again. He lifted up each leg one at a time to look at the socks. "There aren't too many people around here who've got a pair of new socks."

Chapter 5

I knew I couldn't stay too long, for it was a long way back home, and I had to be there for lunch. But I had time to talk with him a little. I looked around for a place where we could sit, but there wasn't any. Now I knew why those out-of-work men I'd seen on my way over had been leaning against factory walls—they hadn't anyplace to sit. So we leaned against the shack wall and talked. "How'd you get the place, Charlie?"

"Some kid was living here. He said he built it himself, but I don't believe that. We met up begging on the same corner. We got into an argument over whose corner it was. After we settled the argument he said I could share the shack with him, it was warmer sleeping two together. We went out begging and shared. But come January he said he couldn't take it anymore, he'd never been so cold in his born days and he lit out for California."

"How did he get out there?"

"Search me. Hitch, I guess. Or hop a freight."

"What's that?"

"You never heard of hopping a freight? The best way is to stand by a long uphill grade. Those long freight trains, a hundred cars, maybe, slow right down to nothing on a

37

grade and you can climb on, easy. Get into a freight car if you can find one unlocked. Otherwise climb into a coal gondola and duck down among the coal."

"Don't you get dirty hiding in coal?"

"Sure you do. When you're poor you get dirty pretty near anything you do."

"It would be best to get into a freight car, I guess."

"Yeah. Sneak into a freight yard and hide in a freight car that looks like it's going somewhere soon. But that's risky. I heard a couple of kids who did that in the dead of winter. Somebody locked the car and then took it up to Montana and left it on a siding for two weeks with the temperature down below zero. When somebody finally opened the car the kids were frozen solid as iron. When they hit 'em with a hammer they rung like a bell. There were big scratch marks up and down the door and their fingers was all bloody, the nails half ripped off, from trying to claw their way out before they froze to death. When you hop a freight you got to be careful it's going someplace warm. Although that isn't always safe, either. Get locked in a freight car down in Georgia when it's 110 degrees in the shade, and you can die from heatstroke."

I could imagine what it must have been like for those poor kids, shrieking as loud as they could and clawing at the door as they got colder and colder. What an awful feeling it must have been. But Charlie told it like it was a joke on them, the kind of thing you've got to expect when you're poor.

"Why would anyone hit them with a hammer?" I asked.

"Search me. Chip the ice off, maybe. Or just fooling around to see what it would sound like."

"Did you ever hop a freight, Charlie?"

"Once. I got sick of being cold all the time, and some kid and I decided we'd go down to Florida and see if we could get work picking oranges. We got caught by the dicks before we were 10 miles out of Chi, and we had to hitch back."

"What are dicks?"

"Detectives. Railroad detectives. They're tough as nails. They'll beat the tar out of you as soon as look at you."

What kept going through my mind was all those afternoons after school I'd spent at Charlie's house back there in third grade playing with his Lionel trains—switching them here and there, pulling them into stations, loading and unloading the little gondolas with the crane. When Charlie hopped that freight to Florida, did he remember those Lionel trains? But I couldn't ask him. There was something else I wanted to ask him, though. "Charlie, what's it like not to have any parents over you, telling you what to do?"

"It wasn't my idea," he said. "I didn't tell my Dad to shoot himself in the head."

"I know," I said. "But what's it like to be able to do whatever you want?"

"What do you mean, do whatever I want, Petey? I can't do anything I want. Can't go to a drugstore for a soda, can't go out to Wrigley Field to see the Cubs play, can't go bike riding, can't go to the movies or listen to the radio."

"Well yes, I get that part of it. But still, you don't have

anyone telling you what to do all the time."

"Everyone tells me what to do. Cops. Railroad dicks. Clerks in stores take one look at me and tell me to get out, even if I've got half a buck to buy something with. Guys bigger than me out here push me away from the fire when they want to get closer, take away my money if they find out I got some. I'm on the bottom of the pile. Know what that feels like, Petey, where everybody you see is above you? The only kick I get out of it is when I run across kids littler than me who I can push around."

I'd never seen that side of it before—it was one more thing to think about. And I was about to say I had to go, when Charlie said, "Uh-oh, here comes Joey."

The guy walking towards us was about 20, kind of tall, thin like the rest of them, red hair that had been hacked off short, probably by himself. He was wearing stiff old canvas pants with paint splotches on them, a heavy blue sweater with the usual holes, and he was chewing a twig from one of the scrawny trees that grew there. He looked me over as he came up. "Where'd you get the swell, Charlie?"

"Leave him alone, Joey. He's a pal of mine."

Joey took the twig out of his mouth and looked me over some more, eyeing me up and down. "Since when is some swell like this a pal of yours?" I wondered if I should make a run for it. With his long legs he'd catch me in a minute.

"I knew him from before," Charlie said. "Leave him alone."

He looked me over some more. "Come out to satisfy

your curiosity about the poor folks, did you? Make sure we got everything we need—nice warm shack, carpet for a door so's you'd hardly notice it when the wind blew through, regular supply of beans and ketchup for breakfast, lunch and dinner; and for variety, ketchup and beans. Well it was mighty good of you to take the trouble." He put the twig back in his mouth and looked me up and down some more.

Maybe I ought to take a chance on running for it anyway. Maybe he was only trying to throw a scare into me and wouldn't chase me. "I came to visit Charlie." I decided not to mention the socks.

"That's right, Joey. Leave him alone."

Joey didn't pay any attention, but took the twig out of his mouth again. "So, what do you think of our little community, eh? Quaint, ain't it? Homey. Rustic charm. Always something doin' here. No end of barn dances, concerts, picture shows, ball games, pee-rades. Why just the other day the fellas was talking about getting up a pee-rade. March downtown just to show everybody what a fine bunch we got here." His eyes were shining and he spit a little when he talked. "Oh yes, we wanted them folks downtown to see how nice things was for us. What fine clothes we got, all the newest styles, shoes that you wouldn't hardly find in the best stores. The fellas was all for it, and had got themselves outfitted with pick handles and such to add a stylish note to their costumes. But the cops got wind of it and come up here and called it off. Said there wasn't no harm in a pee-rade, but they was afraid the fellas might want to take home a little souvenir or two out of them fine shops downtown. The cops said it would run the city a good deal of expense to clean up the broken glass afterwards, and they'd just as soon the fellas stayed out here and enjoyed the rustic charm. Mighty good-hearted, the cops—always happy to see people with their own kind."

He spit through the gap in his front teeth and stuck the twig back in his mouth. "You just wait, sonny. One of these days the fellas are going to come bustin' out of here, cops or no cops, and run through the streets of Chicago smashing and burning and chopping heads off. The French Revolution ain't gonna look like nothin' after that."

I wondered if he'd always been a little off, or had got that way from living in Shacktown. Everywhere people like Joey or Charlie went they saw people who had something they didn't have. They saw people in shops buying cake, eating ice cream sundaes, trying on new shoes. They saw people tooling around in new cars, people going into apartment buildings where the doorman saluted them, people coming out of movies eating popcorn and laughing about the movie they'd just seen. I could see where that would make you a little off after a while.

Suddenly I realized that Joey hated me. I'd never had anyone hate me before. It made me feel scared and ugly. I wanted to get out of there. "I guess I better get home, Charlie."

Joey went on chewing the twig. "He got any money on him, Charlie?"

"No. He isn't as rich as he looks."

"So long, Charlie." I turned and started to walk off, but before I could take more than a couple of steps Joey grabbed me from behind, put one arm around my neck, and pulled me tight against him. Then he shoved his free hand into my right pants pocket and began feeling around. I hated having a strange hand crawling around in my pocket. I struggled to get loose. "Let me go," I shouted.

He squeezed his arm tighter across my neck. "Hold still, you little rat, or I'll choke the life out of you."

"Joey, let him go," Charlie shouted. "He didn't do anything to you." He grabbed hold of Joey's arm and tried to pull it off my neck. I could feel my breath getting short. I took hold of the arm with both hands and tried to pull it loose. It was like pulling on a steel bar.

Now he raised up a foot and pushed Charlie with it, so that Charlie stumbled backwards and fell. Then he switched his hand into my other pants pocket. I took in a big gasp of air and went on squirming. "Let go of me."

"Aha," Joey said. He jerked my Elgin watch out of my pocket, let go of me, and pushed me hard so I fell down too. I jumped up. He was holding my watch up by the strap, swinging it gently in front of him. "As I live and breathe, an Elgin. Good for five bucks at least in a hock shop. Old Joey's gonna have himself a pint of gin and a nice supper tonight."

"Give it back to me. It's mine." My heart was beating real quick, my throat was sore, and I felt dirty from having Joey's hands rummaging around in my pockets. I snatched at the watch, but he jerked it away.

"No, it ain't yours," he snarled. He slipped the watch into his pocket. "Not on your tintype. You didn't sweat your guts out for that watch. That watch come out of the sweat and blood of working folks swinging pickaxes and shovels 10 hours a day in sun hot enough to bake your brains into a Christmas pudding. It come out of old ladies stitching handkerchiefs in some freezing sweatshop until their fingers was bloody from needle pricks. Oh no, that watch ain't yours, sonny boy. It never was. It belongs to the working people, and now we got it back."

My fists were clenched in front of me, my heart was thumping, and sweat was running down my cheeks. "You lousy, rotten—"

"Petey, shut up," Charlie said. "I told you to put it in your underpants."

Joey raised his fist. "I'm a lousy, rotten what, sonny boy?" He stepped towards me and I turned and ran.

Chapter 6

Losing the watch that Gramps had given me hurt a lot.
It had been a big expense for him, Mom had told me,
more than he should have spent; but Gramps and I had
always got along real good and he'd wanted to give me
something nice. I resolved that I wouldn't spend my
allowance on sodas and stuff but would save up until I
could buy one just like it, so he'd never know. What a
dope I'd been to wear that watch out to the shacktown. I
guess you never believe how things really are until you see
for yourself.

But then worse came, for a few days later, when we
were having breakfast, Dad got a phone call from
Gramps. He didn't have a phone out on the farm, but he
could call from the general store up the road. The bank
was going to foreclose.

"Can he save anything, Victor?" Mom said.

"I don't think so, Meg. He owes more than the place
is worth today. You can hardly give a farm away now.
They'll auction the whole place off if they can. The land,
the house, the cattle, farm equipment, furniture."

"Even the furniture?" Mom said. "Your grandmother's
quilts, and the quilt chest your grandfather made for her?"

"They'll leave him his clothes. They aren't worth anything, anyway. And a few tools. There's a law that they can't repossess a workman's tools. He has to be left a way of making a living. Not that it'll do Gramps much good if he hasn't got cows and a cornfield."

I couldn't believe it. "You mean they're going to take away his dishes and everything?" I remembered his old pink-and-white plates with landscape scenes on them— one of mountains, one of a lake, one of a forest, and such. The plates were chipped white at the edges here and there, and some of them had thin curving lines running through them where they'd got broken and Gramps had mended them. Gramps always said those dishes were his wedding present to Grandma and he would always use them. Those chips and cracks were the scars of Grandma's life, just the same as the scars he had on his body where he'd hooked himself on rusty barbed wire, got kicked by a cow, sliced himself with a scythe. I'd been eating off those plates all my life. I loved them. When I was little it was interesting to scrape away the maple syrup to find out if it was the mountain plate, the lake plate, or what.

Dad shrugged. "The dishes aren't worth much. I suppose he'll manage to hang onto some of the stuff."

Mom closed her eyes. "The poor old man. He never got over losing your mother. He never says anything about it, but I know he thinks of her every day. And now this. It'll kill him. He buried her under the cherry tree out back. Who'll keep the weeds off her grave?"

"Dad," I said, "are you going out for the auction?"

"Of course," he said. "I can't leave him to face that alone."

"I want to go with you," I said.

"You don't want to see that, Petey."

"Yes, I do. I want to see things for myself. Especially this."

"No," Mom said. "I don't want Petey to go."

"Why not, Mom?"

"It could be dangerous."

I was puzzled. "What could be dangerous about an auction?"

Mom glanced at Dad. "Petey," Dad said, "Some of the farmers around there are talking about stopping the auction. They've been doing that in some places. Just come in a bunch with their shotguns and drive the sheriff off."

I brightened up. "Will they save the farm? For Gramps?"

Dad shook his head. "I don't know."

"I want to go."

Dad looked at Mom. "We'll see," he said. Then he said, "I have to get going." He put on his jacket and left.

But instead of clearing away the breakfast dishes, Mom sat there, looking at me. "Petey, where were you Saturday morning?"

I went hot and blushed. "Why?"

"Never mind why. Where were you?"

I was stuck. I'd lied about it once and would have to lie about it again. "Playing baseball."

"No you weren't," she said. "You didn't take your baseball glove. I went into your room to put your clean clothes away and I saw your glove lying on your bureau.

What a dope I was. Why hadn't I taken it out and hidden it by the front hedge or something? I prayed Mom wouldn't notice that I wasn't wearing my watch. Feeling hot and sweaty, all I could think of to say was, "Oh."

"You went out to Hooverville to see that boy, didn't you?"

"Yes," I said, looking down at the table.

"After we'd explicitly told you not to."

"Yes."

"Look at me."

I looked up.

"Why, Petey? What was so important that you would break your promise?"

"I never promised."

"That doesn't matter, Petey. You knew you weren't supposed to do it."

"I wanted to see if I could help him," I said. But it wasn't that really. "I wanted to see it for myself. I have a right to know."

"You're 12 years old. You're too young to go to places like that. They're dangerous."

I knew that now, but I didn't want to admit it. "Charlie Henrich is 12 and he lives there, Mom."

She rapped on the table. "I don't want any argument about it. I'm not going to tell your dad. But I want you to drop this idea of going out to the farm for the auction."

"Mom, that's blackmail."

She got up and began clearing the dishes. "Call it what you want, Petey. It's for your own good. There could be violence. It's bad enough your dad has to be there, but he can't leave Gramps to face it alone. But you're not going."

I was stuck. If I tried to talk Dad into letting me go Mom would tell him I'd gone out to shacktown and he'd have to punish me by not taking me out to the auction. There was no way around it.

A week later Gramps called again. The sheriff was coming on Sunday to take the farm. "They're going to hold the auction at noon," Dad explained. "The bank thinks it has a buyer who'll take the whole thing at once. Somebody from Peoria. He's probably representing some big farmer who can afford to pick up land while it's going cheap and hang on to it until times get better. The farmers out there are going to try to stop it. People who've known Gramps all their lives. I don't know how many are involved. Gramps thinks it might be as many as 30. Coming from 20 miles away, some of them. Nobody knows what the sheriff's likely to do."

Mom looked up from her darning. "There'll be violence, Victor."

Dad didn't sit down. He stood in the middle of the living room with his hands clasped in front of him, frowning down into them. "I hope not. I know Sheriff Connolly. We were kids together. I went to school with him. We used to go skinny dipping in the creek all the time." He unclasped his hands and ran them through his hair. "He's sensible. I don't think he'll let things get out of hand."

"Victor, things like this always get out of hand. Tempers are going to rise."

"I hope not. Whatever happens, I have to be there." He took a deep breath. "Meg, I'm taking Petey."

Mom gave me a quick look but went on darning and didn't say anything. I had to tell Dad the truth. I hoped I could make him understand why I'd gone out to shacktown, for I was desperate to go to the farm on Sunday. I stood up, to be more his equal. That was a strange feeling, to be Dad's equal. "I can't go, Dad. I made an agreement with Mom."

He looked at Mom, then at me, then back at Mom. "What's this all about?"

"It's between Petey and me, Victor. Petey has agreed not to go."

I took a deep breath. "I went over to that shacktown to see Charlie Henrich awhile ago. Mom found out. I agreed not to go out to the farm because of it."

Mom bit off a piece of thread from the sock she was darning and began to roll the sock up with its mate. "So you see, Victor, it's settled."

Dad looked at her, and then back at me. "I don't know as anything's settled yet. Petey, we told you, you weren't to go out there. What made you feel you should?"

"Dad, I'm tired of being treated like a little kid. You don't want me to see anything that's going on. You want to keep me out of everything. I'm not a little kid anymore."

"Petey, you were told not to go there," Mom said. "That should have been enough."

Dad waved his hand. "Hold on a minute, Meg. Let's hear him out."

I hadn't expected that; I'd expected him to back up Mom. "Look," I began, "the whole country's falling to pieces, and I was going along like somebody with his eyes closed walking into a buzz saw. Suddenly it turned out that my old friend was living in a shacktown, Dad was taking pay cuts, Gramps was about to lose the farm. It's my life too. I went out to Shacktown to see for myself."

They both looked at me, Mom holding the darning in her hands. Nobody said anything. Then Dad said, "Well, what did you think of it?"

"It was pretty terrible. Charlie lives in this little shack with a mattress on the floor. No sink or toilet or anything. Just this shack."

"Really?" Mom asked. "It's that bad? The poor child."

"I don't think Charlie's a child anymore," I said.

"Meg, there's something to what Petey says. In bad times these kids are having to grow up fast."

Mom let go of her darning. She sighed and blinked her eyes. "I've always hoped that somehow, I could see my children grow up happy."

"I'm not a child," I said. "I'm almost 13. I don't want to be talked to like a child anymore."

"Oh, Petey," Mom said. She put her fists into her eyes

and rubbed them. She wasn't crying, just sad. "I didn't want you to grow up this quick. I wanted you to be young and safe as long as you could—play baseball, read Oz books, pick blueberries, and swim in Gramps's creek." She shook her head. "I guess nobody can stay young when hard times come." She put her darning away in her round wicker sewing basket and stood up. "All right, Victor, you can take him with you on Sunday. But I hope you're not doing something you'll have to live with for the rest of your life." She put her sewing basket on the living room table. "I've had enough of the Depression for one night. I'm going to bed."

Chapter 7

It was sort of like going on a fishing trip. Sometimes Dad would take Steve and me up north to the lakes fishing. We'd get up real early in the morning, when it was still dark out. The house all quiet, no noises of cars from the street. Mom would still be asleep. Steve would come over for breakfast. Dad would always cook the same thing—scrambled eggs and fried ham. He said it was the only thing he knew how to cook. Then off we'd go, with the sky getting gray in the east as sunrise started to come.

It was just like that on Sunday, except it wasn't going to be much fun. Dad and I didn't talk much, just about the weather and if I needed to take a sweater. Then we left and drove off in the Buick, the sun still not up, gray light in the empty streets of Chicago.

Gramps's farm was out near Peru. It was exactly 80 miles. Even though we'd driven out there dozens of times, Dad always took the mileage. It seemed to please him each time it came out to exactly 80 miles as we turned into the farm lane.

We got out of the city and onto the country roads that ran across the state through farms and small towns, the sky slowly turning from gray to blue as the sun came up behind us. In the fields along the way, the corn was coming up green, not yet a foot high. "Look at that," Dad said. "We've got a glut of food in America, and all over the country people are going to bed hungry at night. Did you read about that farm strike in Sioux City, where the strikers attacked the ones who were trying to get their milk to market, and dumped it in the ditches? And there's your friend Charlie, desperate for a quarter to buy a fried-egg sandwich."

"What did they dump the milk out for?" I asked.

"The basic problem for the farmers, Gramps included, is that they can't get a good enough price for their milk—can't get enough to make the farm pay. So here and there the farmers get together and set a higher price on their milk. If the bottlers won't pay, they dump it. The problem is that there's always a few who're willing to sell at the lower price."

"They shouldn't do that, should they, Dad?"

"I don't know. Sometimes you can't blame a fellow for it. Maybe he's got a sick wife who needs expensive medicines. Maybe he's got a lot of hungry kids." He took his eyes off the road to give me a quick glance. "You know, Petey, things weren't so hot for the farmers even when times were good, in the 20s before the Depression. Prices for wheat, milk, hogs were too low even then. For a lot of farmers, the Depression just made a bad situation worse. Not all, but a lot of them. Gramps never had much money, you know."

"Whose fault is it, then? What's the explanation for it?"

"Maybe it isn't anybody's fault. Maybe it's just the nature of things. Maybe we're always going to have these business cycles, where you have good times and hard times coming along one after the other. We've had hard times before, although I admit they weren't so bad. Gramps remembers the 1893 crisis, when his own father almost lost the farm."

"It's got to be somebody's fault, Dad. It isn't like a tornado. It's people doing it."

Dad laughed. "Petey, some of the smartest men in the country have spent the last four years trying to figure out what went wrong. We're not going to find an answer this morning. I've still got faith in capitalism. It worked before and it'll work again. But it's clear that somebody's got to do something. Businessmen haven't been able to solve it any more than the government has. Roosevelt has a scheme for paying farmers to cut down on production— grow fewer hogs, produce less milk, and so forth. Create artificial shortages to force farm prices up. They hope it'll start an upward spiral. If farmers make some money, they'll order new farm equipment, we'll hire back some of the people we had to lay off, the workers will have a little money in their pockets to buy new shoes for the kids, a roast beef for Sunday dinner. Maybe it'll work. I don't know."

The whole thing worried me a lot. "Dad, what if things get worse? What if you get laid off too?"

He shook his head. "That isn't going to happen, son. Mr. O'Connor says I've always been loyal to him, he'll always be loyal to me."

The sun was now up, and the countryside bright. But now I was noticing things that I hadn't noticed before—the farmhouses so weather-beaten that gray wood showed through the white paint, barns all gray with only patches of red here and there, chimneys crooked, roofs on chicken houses sagging. There was a sadness over the land, and it was making me sad too. I wondered what Uncle Jim would think if we lost the farm. Maybe he didn't care anymore, he left so long ago.

The countryside began to get familiar. We crossed a wooden bridge over the stream that wound along down to Gramps's house, passed Tyler's General Store where Gramps bought nails, kerosene, soap, and made his phone calls. Then we turned into the farm lane. Dad looked at the speedometer. "Eighty miles, exactly," he said. I wondered if he'd ever say it again.

Gramps was alone, sitting at the old wooden kitchen table, smooth as oil from I don't know how many years of scrubbing. Gramps was tall and thin, his face the color of an old baseball glove from being out in the weather all his life. He had on overalls, an old blue shirt, boots, and a red bandanna around his neck. Mom said I was built like him. I hoped so—a lanky build was good for a shortstop.

He stood up when we came in and shook hands, first Dad and then me. "Cup of coffee, boys?"

"Sure," Dad said. Gramps got out three mugs and poured the coffee. At home Mom wouldn't have let me have coffee, but Dad didn't say anything. Instead, he asked, "How're you feeling, Pa?" When we were on the farm Dad always talked a little more the way farm people did.

"Purty good for an old geezer."

"When's the sheriff coming?"

"Noon," Gramps said. "He came out the other day and explained everything. He said he was mighty sorry about it, he had to do it a dozen times in the past year, he always hated it, but the law was the law. He said he hoped I wouldn't raise a fuss. I told him, 'Connolly, I knowed you since you was four years old. You think a man ain't gonna make a fuss when you put him off'n his farm where he lived for 72 years? Well, you got another think comin'."

Gramps was the quiet kind, never did a lot of talking. Grandma had been the opposite, chattering away all the time. Gramps said it was all right, she did enough talking for the two of them. But he was speaking up now.

The men began coming at around 11 o'clock. Some of them came in horse and wagon—pairs of horses, wagon wheels creaking, caked with mud, manure, hayseeds around the axle hubs and on the tailgates. Most of them had trucks, stake bodies mainly, that they used for haying and carting milk cans to town. Trucks 10, 15 years old. Not a new one among them. They parked the trucks out back in the barnyard and along the edge of the cornfield, taking care not to drive over any of the corn. They were dressed like Gramps in blue denim overalls, rubber boots, big red handkerchiefs around their necks.

Gramps stood on the front porch. He'd brought out a

little green wooden table and had put a jug of cider and
two or three jelly glasses on it. The farmers would come
up to him, two or three at a time. They'd shake hands and
Gramps would say, "Hello Ben, hello Jack, nice of you to
come." He'd pour them glasses of cider, which they'd toss
off at a gulp, and then go down off the porch to stand
around talking quietly, some chewing tobacco and
spitting into the grass.

Dad and I stood down at one end of the porch to be
out of the way. But some of the farmers came over to us,
shook Dad's hand and said, "How's things, fella?"

Dad told me, "I went to school with a lot of these
people. Knew 'em since we were tads." I liked it that Dad
had so many friends there.

Then a farm truck pulled up the lane and eased into
the front yard. The crowd made way for it. It pulled along
until it was under the big maple tree with the tire swing.
A farmer got out of the truck carrying a coil of rope.
Everybody turned to watch him. He climbed into the
back and then onto the roof of the cab. He shook loose a
few coils of rope, twirled the end, and flung it upwards. It
arced, clunked against a branch, and fell back. The farmer
swore, and somebody called out, "You cain't pitch better'n
that, Osborne, they'll send you back down to the
minors."

There was a chuckle. Osborne swore again. He twirled
the rope and flung it upwards once more. This time it
arced over the branch and dropped down the other side.
Now we could see that there was a hangman's noose

dangling at the end of the rope, about 15 feet off the ground. Osborne flung the slack onto the ground, climbed down after it, and fastened it around the trunk of the tree. The noose hung there, swinging slowly around. I'd never seen a hangman's noose before, except in the movies. It looked mighty scary hanging there, and I couldn't take my eyes off it. What would it be like to see somebody hanging from it, his eyes bulging and his tongue sticking out?

"Don't worry, Petey," Dad said. "They're just trying to throw a scare into people."

"I thought so," I said. But I wasn't so sure.

He put his hand on my shoulder. "If there's any trouble, I want you to duck inside the house and stay away from windows. Hear me?"

"Okay," I said. I wasn't going to, though. I wanted to see everything for myself.

Then we saw the sheriff's car coming down the lane— a white sedan with *Sheriff Putnam County* in red letters on the door. Behind it were two state police cars. They stopped about a hundred feet away, and out popped six state police carrying shotguns, the sheriff, and a man in a suit. The sheriff wore ordinary clothes, with high-cut boots and a cowboy hat. They walked down the lane in single file, the sheriff leading the way, the man in the suit in the middle. The farmers on the lawn made a path for them up to the house. They went on through in single file, up onto the porch, right past where Dad and I were standing, so close I could have touched them. They stood there in a line on the porch facing the mob of farmers on the lawn, three state troopers to either side, the sheriff and the man in the suit in the middle. The troopers stood straight, the shotguns hanging in the crooks of their arms.

I looked at Gramps. He was down near the other end of the porch, next to the little green table with the cider jug on it, standing straight as a soldier, his face still. But his hands were clenched at his sides, and his thumbs were rubbing back and forth across his fists. I was pretty sure I knew what he was thinking. He wasn't thinking about the auction, the sheriff, the noose: he was thinking about Grandma.

Dad touched me on the shoulder. "Let's get off of here," he said. "No need to be in the line of fire."

"What about Gramps?"

"Leave him be," Dad said. "Let him think his own thoughts."

We slipped off the porch and stood on the lawn a little apart from the mob of farmers. I looked up at the state troopers and hated them. They were scary to look at, standing straight and stern with the shotguns crooked under their arms. I hated them for being there.

Now the sheriff took a step forward to the edge of the porch, so everybody could see him clearly. He pointed up to the hangman's noose dangling over the crowd of farmers. "What blame fool put that up there?"

Nobody said anything. The sheriff looked around the crowd from one face to the next. He knew them all. "Frank Osborne, that there's your truck parked under that tree, ain't it?"

Osborne shook his head. "Purely coincidence, Sheriff. Must of been the elves who done it."

There was a dry, hard chuckle from the crowd. The sheriff put his hands on his hips, his right hand resting just behind the butt of his pistol. "Now you boys know you ain't gonna hang nobody this morning. So stop being a bunch of blame fools and use your common sense. Nobody hates it worse than me to see Pappy Williamson lose this here farm. Me and his boy Vic swum naked as jays many a time in that creek out beyond the cornfield. Stole raspberries off'n Pappy's bushes afterwards and come in lyin' about it, our faces smeared up red as paint. He looked over at Dad. "Ain't that right, Vic?"

"That's right," Dad said. Just that, nothing more.

The sheriff dropped his hands off his hips and let them hang by his side. "I'd sooner sell off my own place as Pappy's. But the law's the law. Now I want all you boys who ain't got any business here to climb into your trucks and go on home."

Nobody stirred; nobody moved. "You heard what I said." He reached inside his shirt and took out a piece of paper. "This here's a court order. Anybody who ain't got any business here this morning, you're in contempt of court if you don't skedaddle, pronto."

Nobody stirred; nobody moved; nobody said anything. They were all still as frozen woods. My heart was pounding and my breath was short. It was the stillness of them that got me more than anything else.

They weren't human beings anymore but a huge something ready to pounce.

The sheriff turned to the man in the suit and said something in a low voice. The man took a handkerchief out of his breast pocket, wiped his forehead, and tucked the handkerchief away again. The sheriff took a piece of paper out of his pocket and said, "All right folks. This here's an order from the court to auction this property. Nice farm here, 20 head of cattle, barn and equipment in good order." He paused and looked around. "What am I bid?"

A wisp of silence hung in the air. Then Frank Osborne said good and loud, "Mighty poor specimen of a farm, I'd say. I'd be doin' Pappy Williamson a favor just to take it off'n his hands. But just to make it all legal, I bid a dollar."

There was another low, dry chuckle. There wasn't much fun in it for any of them, for some of them were likely to be in this same boat soon enough. Silence fell again. "All right," Sheriff Connolly said. "Let's cut out the foolishness. I ain't acceptin' that bid."

"You got to," somebody shouted. "That's the law."

"I still ain't acceptin' it." He looked around the crowd. "Anyone out there got the guts to make a legitimate offer on this here farm?"

For a minute nobody said anything. Then the man in the suit took out his handkerchief, wiped his face again, and stuffed the handkerchief back in his breast pocket. He took a deep breath, and in a high, quavery voice said,

"Sheriff, I place a bid of $2,000."

Nobody moved. I looked at Gramps. He was still standing straight as a soldier, staring at the man in the suit, his fists clenched, his thumbs circling round and round. The silence went on. Finally Frank Osborne said loudly, "That bid ain't acceptable, neither."

There was a murmur, like bees stirring in a honeysuckle vine. "That's right," a voice said, and other voices popped out of the crowd, "Right, you heard it, right."

The man in the suit looked at the sheriff. The sheriff put his hands on his hips again, his right hand just behind the butt of his pistol. The state troopers shifted a little. "Now boys," Sheriff Connolly said, "That's a reasonable bid. I got to accept it." He looked around. "Any more bids? Anyone want to raise on that?"

There came the bee hum again, and then a shout. "I say we run these buzzards out of here."

The sheriff raised his hands. "Boys, I don't like this no more'n you do, but the law's the law. You ain't gonna solve anything by taking the law into your own hands. Now this here auction is over. I'm askin' you nice, just get in your trucks and go home."

"Come on, what's the matter with you fellas?" Osborne shouted. He snapped his head around to glare here and there at the crowd. "Sam, Jack, Eddie Hoskins, you fellas gonna let these buzzards run Pappy Williamson off'n his own place where he was born and raised?"

There was a rustle and a movement in the crowd of

farmers, a sort of leaning forward. Up on the porch the state troopers, their shotguns raised, were looking at Sheriff Connolly. The man in the suit shrunk back, but he didn't run. The sheriff raised his hands again. "Go easy. We don't want no bloodshed here today."

The bee hum was loud and crackling here and there with words. Suddenly Frank Osborne jumped out in front of the crowd. He stretched out his arm and pointed his finger at the sheriff. "Connolly, you tellin' me you'd shoot down in cold blood some fellas you known all your stinkin' life? I wouldn't spit on the best part of you." He turned his face to the crowd. "Come on," he shouted.

The sheriff snapped his head around to look at Gramps. "Pappy Williamson, you don't want no bloodshed out here today, do you? You tell these here fellas —"

But Frank Osborne was charging toward the porch. Behind him the mob broke and poured forward, shouting. Dad grabbed me by the collar and dragged me backwards. I lost my balance and fell back, my arms wheeling. He dragged me back 20 feet, dropped me, and raced towards Gramps, who was standing in the same spot, still straight as a soldier, his thumbs working over his fists. I jumped onto my feet. The farmers were swarming all over the porch, tussling with the state troopers, who were using their shotguns like rams, trying to break themselves loose. If one of the shotguns went off it would blow a hole in somebody as big as a fist. There came a crash as one of the windows was smashed, glass, wood, and all. Now Dad was on the porch, holding Gramps by the shirt front, trying to drag him away. But Gramps had hold of one of the porch posts and was hanging on.

Then the police burst out of the mob, half pushing, half carrying the man in the suit. They shoved their way clear and ran across the lawn. One sleeve of the man's suit was ripped off, and dangled down over his arm like an elephant's trunk. The farmers stood on the porch, shaking their fists after the troopers, jeering and hooting like owls. In a moment the police cars were swinging around in Gramps's cornfield, crushing down the young corn, and then heading down the farm lane and out of sight.

Chapter 8

On Tuesday morning, as I was coming around the corner to our street on my way home from school, I saw Charlie Henrich. He was standing a little way off the sidewalk under a big maple tree, sort of hidden in the shadows. He was wearing the socks I'd given him, had taped up his shoes so that his toes didn't stick out, and had combed his hair a little. I figured he was afraid he might run into some of the kids he used to know and wanted to look as good as he could. He still had the jacket with the torn pocket, but he was wearing a blue work shirt instead of the sweater with the holes in it.

"Hey, Charlie," I said.

He stepped out of the shadows a little way but kept looking around to see who might be coming. "Listen, Petey, I'm sorry about Joey taking your watch. I hope you're not mad at me."

"It wasn't your fault, Charlie. I should have put it down in my underpants the way you said."

"I was afraid you'd be mad at me."

"I'm mad at that guy Joey, not at you. I'm saving up to buy a new one. Where'd you get the new shirt?"

"I borrowed it from some kid out there."

I wondered if I could get away with giving him one of my shirts. I had four. I figured Mom would notice. I took Charlie home with me. Mom knew who it was right away, and she laid an after-school snack on the kitchen table about twice as big as she normally did—a big fat peanut butter and jelly sandwich instead of a couple of cookies, and two glasses of milk. And when she saw how Charlie gobbled down his sandwich, she put the bread and peanut butter on the table and told us to help ourselves. So we had another sandwich. "I like your mom," Charlie said. "She's real nice."

I figured it might make him feel better if he knew that we had troubles, too, and were more like him than it looked. "They almost foreclosed on my grampa's farm. Some of the other farmers came around and ran the sheriff off. There were six state cops there with shotguns, but they didn't dare shoot anybody."

"Mostly cops like to whack you around with their nightsticks," Charlie said. "They might get into trouble if they shoot you, but if they beat you up they can always say you were in a fight with some other guy and they were just trying to break it up."

"Gramps might lose his farm, anyway, according to Dad. He says it isn't the bank's money, it belongs to the people who put it in the bank. The thing is, Roosevelt's got some New Deal program to help farmers. Dad says if it goes through soon enough we might save the farm."

"The government never did anything for anybody that I could see except push people around," Charlie said. He wasn't much interested in our problems; to him, we were

67

pretty rich. I guessed that was why he didn't seem bothered at all about taking charity from us. If it had been me, taking charity from Eddie Driscoll's mom or Johnny Bright's, I'd have been embarrassed; but Charlie just sat there happily eating his peanut butter sandwich. But he'd taken the trouble to borrow a clean shirt from somebody before he'd come to see me, so he must have been a little embarrassed about who he was now.

"I've got to ask Mom something," I said. I went out to the living room, where Mom was taking down the curtains to wash them, and asked her if she'd sew up the pocket to Charlie's jacket. She said she would. I went back to the kitchen. Charlie was sitting there chewing on the last of his sandwich, but he seemed sort of bent forward like he'd just sat down, and I had got a funny feeling that he'd just dashed back to his chair. "Mom said she'd sew up your coat."

"Would she really?"

"Sure. She said it would only take a minute."

"Can I go to the bathroom first?"

"Sure," I said. I showed him where, and in a couple of minutes he came back holding the jacket. Mom sewed it up. Then he said he had to go, he was supposed to meet somebody. "I just came over to make sure you weren't mad at me about Joey." I wished he hadn't said that in front of Mom, but she didn't say anything. I went outside with him. When he reached the sidewalk he said, "Petey, I didn't borrow this shirt from any kid. I stole it off a carton in front of a store. I couldn't stand looking the way

I did anymore. The guy was sitting there on a stool watching me, but some women started asking him about something and as soon as he turned his head I snatched a shirt and ran. I was around the corner before he could do anything."

He looked me full in the face, daring me to scold him. But I wouldn't do that. "Maybe I'd have done the same in your place."

Then he said he'd come again sometime. "I just wanted to make sure you weren't mad at me about Joey."

We said goodbye, and he turned and walked away. But he was walking a little funny, and I knew that he'd got something tucked down in his pants. He snatched something up when I'd gone out of the kitchen and shoved it into his jacket pocket; and when I'd told him that Mom would sew his jacket for him he'd gone into the bathroom and shoved whatever it was into his pants. It made me mad, a little; but how could you get real mad at somebody who lived the way he did?

May passed and June came, and Ruth came home from college. Her first night home, she came into my room and sat on the edge of my bed, her chin in her hands. "Are you going back to college?" I said.

"No," she said. "I can't. Dad says he can't afford it." She shook her head so that her brown hair flew. "I hate this Depression. I hate it. Why did it have to happen?"

"A kid I used to know back in second grade is living in a shack in the Hooverville."

She breathed out a long sigh. "Yeah, I know. A lot of

people are worse off than we are. A girl I knew at college had to quit in the middle of the semester because her dad lost all his money and drowned himself."

"This kid's dad killed himself too."

She lay down on my bed and put her hands over her eyes. "I loved college. Lots of boys, parties after the football games. Or somebody's mom would send her a cake and a bunch of us girls would get together in her room and sing and eat the cake."

"I thought you were supposed to be studying."

"Don't start in with that, Petey. You sound just like Mom. I got all-right grades."

"What're you going to do?"

"I have to get a job. I was hoping I could get some kind of an office job—secretary to somebody. Mom says to forget it, you have to know how to type and take dictation. She says I should take a secretarial course. Meanwhile I have to get some kind of a job as a waitress or in the dime store as a clerk. Beeeyaah. I hate this Depression."

"I guess I'll spend the summer on the farm helping Gramps," I said. I would have to be a real help, too, Dad had told me. Gramps was getting on and couldn't get the hay in all by himself anymore. "You won't be going to the farm then? You'll stay here with Dad?"

She took her hands off her eyes and turned her head to look at me. "Didn't they tell you, Petey? We have to move. We aren't going to live here anymore."

I sat there, shocked. "I don't believe it," I said. "They never said anything about it."

"It only got definite a couple of weeks ago. Dad's been hoping he could find a way around it."

I sat there staring at her. I'd never lived anywhere else. It seemed unbelievable that all of a sudden we wouldn't be living here anymore. "What happened?"

She shrugged. "Allied Farm Implements is losing money. Dad's had all these pay cuts. He's making less than half of what he did two or three years ago. He can't make the mortgage payments. Right now he's six months behind. We have to sell the house for whatever we can get before the bank takes it."

"Where are we going to live, Ruth?"

"In some crummy little apartment somewhere."

I still couldn't believe it, but it was true. When I asked Dad and Mom about it, they said they kept hoping they'd find a way out of it. Mom and I would go out to the farm for the summer, Ruth would look for a job, and she and Dad would come out on Saturday afternoons, when Dad got off work. We'd stay in the house until Dad could sell it; then we'd move.

Steve was out of college too. He drove around in his Packard to say goodbye. "I'm going to California to work with the grapefruit pickers. I'll be tied up with one of the unions out there."

"Going to raise up the workers over us filthy capitalists, eh Steve?" Dad said.

Steve grinned. "I hope so."

"What's Mort think of it?"

"Pop's been better about it than you'd think. Let's face it: basically I'm out to tear down everything he's spent his

71

life building up. Not him, personally, of course, but the system he's part of. He might have disowned me, but he hasn't."

"What would you have done if he had, Steve?" Dad said.

"It wouldn't matter, Uncle Vic. I'm not going to take any more money from him. I'm going to make my own way. I should have done it a couple of years back. If I want to go back to college I'll find a way to pay for it myself. Uncle Vic, there's a revolution coming in this country. The workers are going to take over, the way they have in the Soviet Union. It's all going to be different. I hope you don't mind me saying this, Uncle Vic, but you and Pop are irrelevant. You're part of the old system. There's a new world coming."

For a minute Dad frowned, but then he smiled. "You're going to line Mort and me against a wall and shoot us, the way they did to the nobility in Russia?"

Steve grinned again. "No, we won't do that, Uncle Vic. We'll put you to work on the shop floor like everybody else."

Dad shook his head. "Steve, I appreciate that you're thinking about these things, and I'm the last one to defend what a lot of the money boys have done in the past. We know that some of the bankers got careless, we know that some of them were outright crooked. Look at what happened at Merchants National, where Bill Henrich worked. Some of the executives there were lending themselves the bank's money to invest in the stock market, figuring the market would keep going up and they'd pay the loans back when they'd made their pile. When the market crashed instead, they were stuck. The bank folded up, and some of them went to jail." Dad looked at me. "Petey, I'm not saying that Bill Henrich was guilty, but somebody was." He looked back at Steve. "So I agree that maybe the government ought to keep a closer eye on the banks, the stock brokers, the money people more than they did in the past. Roosevelt's going to introduce a lot of controls over business, and I'm sure that some of them are long overdue. But a revolution? No." He shook his head firmly. "I'm with those people on the shop floor every day. They aren't talking revolution. Better pay, shorter hours, sure. Better working conditions— lockers, showers, a canteen, coffee breaks—sure. But a revolution, no. A lot of these working people aren't even interested in joining a union. They don't trust the unions."

"Uncle Vic, maybe what they tell you and what they tell me is different."

"Maybe so," Dad said. "But I doubt it. I hear too much of it too often."

Then Steve had to go. I went outside with him. "I wish you were staying in Chicago, Steve."

He put his arm around my shoulder. "I'm going to miss all of you," he said. "But there's too much going on in California. I want to be part of it." He climbed into the Packard and drove away.

Mom and I spent the summer helping Gramps with the farm. So far, the bank hadn't tried to foreclose again. Dad said they weren't eager to take farms—weren't enough buyers around. Gramps's bank was probably hoping the government would put through a scheme to help the farmers pay off their loans. We got the hay into the barn, the corn into the silo. Mom canned enough tomatoes, beans, berries, watermelon pickles, and peach preserves to last Gramps through the winter. "It might be his last winter out here," she said. "At least let him eat well."

We went back home when school started in the fall. Ruth had got a job as a counter girl in a cafeteria in the Loop. It was a terrible job—nine hours a day, $17 a week. And it took her six weeks to get it too. Poor Ruth, she'd never had a real job before—worked on the farm some, but mostly that was working with Grandma in the vegetable garden a little, or helping with the canning and the watermelon pickles. Working in a cafeteria was different. She came home so tired sometimes she'd go to bed right after supper. "They rush you something awful. You never get a minute to sit down. That Mr. Gilkey, he stands by the cash register watching, and if he sees you take three seconds to stretch, he pounces on you. The girls all hate him and make fun of him behind his back, but they're afraid of him because he'll fire you in a second. They make fun of me, too, because of the way I talk. They call me Miss Stuck Up and Betty Co-ed. They say *ain't* and *gonna*. And all they talk about is their boyfriends."

"Maybe you'll get used to it," I said.

"I hope I get an office job soon. I'm starting night school next week."

But she didn't get an office job, and after awhile she got used to the cafeteria. She even got to be friends with some of the other girls and would go out with them after work sometimes. "It's funny, Petey, a year ago I wouldn't have been caught dead going out with girls like that. But when you get to know them, they're pretty good kids."

Chapter 9

That winter we lost our house. One afternoon when I came home from school Mom was in the living room, taking her figurines of shepherdesses and animals out of the cabinet, wrapping them in newspaper, and packing them into a cardboard carton.

"What're you doing, Mom?"

She turned around to look at me. "What do you think I'm doing, Petey? We're moving next week."

I stood there, my mind sort of blank. "We're really moving?"

"Petey, for goodness sake, we've been talking about it for a long while."

It was true: they had. They didn't keep things from me anymore, and there had been discussions about how much we might get for the house, how much we could afford to pay for an apartment, and so on. But it hadn't stuck. It had just been talk. "I didn't think it would really happen," I said. Now I noticed that the living-room pictures were gone—the picture of Notre Dame cathedral in Paris that had hung behind Dad's chair, the rabbit huddled in the snow among the tree trunks over the bookcase, the photos of Mom and Uncle Mort's parents, who were dead, that had been by the door to the dining room. They were leaning against a wall, tied in a bundle with twine.

Mom stood there, holding a half-wrapped figurine of a sheep in her hands. "Poor Petey," she said. "You just didn't want to believe it, did you?"

"I thought things like this happened to other people, they didn't happen to us." I felt awful, sort of dizzy and strange, my stomach hollow. Suddenly I realized I was about to cry. I didn't want to, not in front of Mom. A kind of gasp came out of my mouth. I sucked in a mouthful of air. "I'm going to my room for a while," I said.

Mom gave me 15 minutes to calm down, and then I heard her footsteps coming up the stairs. I was lying face down on my bed. I wiped off my face with my pillow case, rolled over onto my back and stared up at the ceiling. She came in, carrying a glass of milk and a couple of doughnuts on a plate. She put them down on my desk, sat down on the edge of the bed, and put her hand on my forehead. "You feel warm," she said.

"I feel terrible. Why did it have to happen to us?"

"It's happened to a lot of people," she said, brushing my hair down. "Dad's tried everything he could think of. This house meant a lot to him, too. A farm boy who'd made his way up in the world and could afford a decent car, a nice house for his family. It meant a whole lot to him that he'd done well, and now he's losing it through no fault of his own."

"I can't get used to it," I said. "I've lived here all my life. I figured I always would."

She went on brushing down my hair. "You would have

moved out in a few years, anyway. Gone off to college if things had been normal. You'll reach the time when you won't want to live with your family."

"That's someday. Not now."

"Someday always comes." She sighed. "We didn't realize you'd dismissed it all from your mind. We were surprised that you haven't been more upset about it. We should have realized that you hadn't accepted it could happen."

"I still don't," I said.

She stopped brushing my hair. "All right, Petey, we have to face up to it. None of us like it any more than you do. We're going to take a lot of stuff out to the farm and store it there. I want you to go through your things and throw away anything you don't have any use for. Pack up everything else for storage except what you really need. Now eat your snack, and then come down and get a couple of cartons."

So I did, and slowly I began to pack, that afternoon, the next afternoon, the afternoon after that. I started with my books because I figured it would be easier to decide about them. I'd kept them all, right back to when I was little. I put into the discard pile a couple of A-B-C books and some picture books like *Chicken Little* and *Willie the Whale*. It took me awhile to get the books done because I kept stopping to look through ones I hadn't read for years. There were some I'd completely forgotten about. Some of them didn't really mean much to me. But there were some old ones I really liked when I was a kid, like *The Pearl and the Pumpkin*, and one by Edward Lear. Would I ever read them again? No, probably not. So I put them in the discard pile

78

too. Mom said she'd give them to a settlement house so other kids could enjoy them too.

Once I got the books done, I turned to the other stuff. There was my first baseball glove that Steve had given me for my sixth birthday. I couldn't even get it on my hand anymore, but I had a feeling for that glove, and I sat there on the edge of my bed for a long while looking at it.

Then suddenly I understood what I was doing: I was getting rid of my childhood. I was chipping it off bit by bit and throwing it away. That person who'd had *Chicken Little* read to him, who'd tried to catch a ball with that little glove, who'd collected that beach glass along Lake Michigan, who'd sent away for that magnetic ring—that person was gone. Once he'd lived in that room, read those books, held up that beach glass to the light so it'd flash spots of color on the walls. But he was gone, had disappeared like a firefly twinkling out in the dark. Once I understood this, I felt better. I wasn't going to be a kid anymore, I had to grow up some, so I tossed the old baseball glove into the discard pile.

A week later we moved into an apartment. It was in an area of two- and three-story wooden buildings with stores on the ground floors, apartments above. There was a cigar store on the corner, an auto supply store with mufflers and seat covers in the windows across from us, and a Woolworth's Five and Dime in between. Our apartment was over a grocery store. You went down the side street, through a little wooden door, and up a flight of gray wooden stairs. Dad said, "It's all I could find that we could afford in the same school district. It's only temporary. As soon as we sell the house we'll get our finances straightened around and find something better."

Even so, the first time I walked up those gray stairs under the naked lightbulb, my heart sank. When I saw the apartment I felt worse. The living room was about half the size of our old one. The linoleum in the kitchen was coming up in places, the stove was old and had a dent in the oven door, the refrigerator had rust spots on the side. From the windows you didn't see trees and grass, but the auto supply store in the front, and a yard with clothes lines crisscrossing it out back. Ruth and I would have to share a room.

But Dad's Morris chair sat in the living room, the pictures of Notre Dame cathedral and the rabbit huddled in the snow were on the walls, Mom's figurines were in the cabinet. That was something, at least, even though it was strange to see our things in a different place.

Ruth and I went into our room. "What do you think of the place?" I said.

"It's hideous. I hate it."

"Maybe we'll get used to it."

"That's the trouble," she said. "We will." She shrugged. "Petey, most of the girls I work with are worse off. You should see some of their places. A couple of the girls don't even have their own bedrooms. Their little brothers and sisters have the bedroom. One of them sleeps on the sofa every night, the other one in two easy chairs shoved face to face. They keep their clothes in cardboard cartons. They'd love to have a bedroom to share with somebody."

I sat down on my bed. "I guess I'll get used to it," I said. "I guess we were coddled before."

Mom came in. "Here are some coat hangers," she said. "I know the closet isn't very big, but you'll have to manage."

"I don't have any decent clothes anymore, anyway," Ruth said.

"I don't want to hear any of that," Mom said. "Your father is worried enough as it is over the company. He put half his life into rising up there, and it's all they can do to keep going. Some nights he can hardly sleep. I'll hear him get up at two o'clock in the morning and go out to the kitchen for a glass of milk. I'll wake up, at four and he'll be sitting there in the kitchen with a pencil and piece of paper trying to work out something to pull the company through."

"Mom, is he likely to get laid off?" I asked.

She looked at us. "He says he won't," she said.

So we settled in, and bit by bit I got used to it, until one day, suddenly, I realized living there had become normal to me: the old house belonged to another life, a life I used to have but didn't have anymore.

It wasn't just the house that was gone: Steve was gone too. We heard about him when we visited Uncle Mort and Aunt Mae—mostly it was Aunt Mae who talked about where he was and what he was doing. He'd been working with the fruit pickers and was getting toughened up, but he was thinking of trying something else. I wished he'd write me, even a postcard, but Aunt Mae said he didn't have much time to write—all they got from him were postcards.

But then we got a long letter from him, which Dad read to us at supper.

Dear Williamsons,

I'm out in San Francisco now. Trying to organize the farm workers was frustrating. Every time we held a meeting the sheriffs would turn up. A lot of the workers were scared they'd lose their jobs if they were caught trying to organize a union. When the picking season ended I gave up on it and came to San Francisco. I'm trying to get work as a longshoreman loading ships. These poor guys have really got it bad. You have to "shape-up" every morning—that means go down to the docks, and if you're lucky, some foreman will pick you for a crew that day. So only a few favorites get to work all the time. Most of these guys don't make more than 40 or 50 bucks a month. On top of it, some of the foremen want you to kick back 10 or 20 percent of your pay. This, for the second most dangerous kind of work in the U.S., next to mining. So you can understand why the longshoremen are angry—enraged is more like it. There's a fellow out here, Harry Bridges—maybe you've read about him in the papers. They say he's a Communist, and I guess he probably is. He's got the guys behind him. We're going to strike. It'll be tough, and there's likely to be violence, but it's what I came out here for. I didn't get work today which is why I have time to write and am down to my last 50 cents, but for the first time since I got out to the Coast I feel like I've got in on something that matters. We're going to change things. The men feel it. They're fed to the teeth with a capitalist system that doesn't pay a living wage. I'm mighty proud to be one of them. Keep watching the newspapers—you'll see.

When Dad got finished reading the letter, we sat quiet for a minute. Then Mom said, "I hope Steve hasn't gone Communist."

"Pretty close to it, I should think," Dad said.

Then Ruth said, "Why does being for the workers make Steve a Communist? I wish we had a union where I work. Look at the way they treat us. Seventeen dollars a week and only a half-hour break for lunch, and you might not get that until three o'clock. You're starving by then, but let Gilkey catch you sneaking a roll and he'll fire you on the spot."

Dad frowned. "There's a difference between treating your workers fairly and being a Communist. I agree, the shipowners shouldn't be paying the longshoremen 50 dollars a month. That's not right. But I have to say, we're not paying our people much more than that. We can't. Steve ought to understand that all businessmen aren't wicked taskmasters grinding down on the workers. Most of us would jump for joy if we got to the point where we could give our people raises. But we don't want things here the way they are in Russia, with police knocking on your door in the middle of the night and shipping you off to Siberia just because you criticized the government. Steve ought to remember that under Communism he wouldn't be free to express his opinions this way."

Chapter 10

One day in April I came home from school, and there was Dad sitting in the Morris chair in the living room. His jacket was flung on the sofa, his tie was loose, and he was holding a bottle of beer in his lap and staring down at it. It was strange to see him home on a weekday, especially drinking a beer, for Dad never drank much—a bottle of beer on a picnic, or maybe one after work on a real hot summer's day.

"Are you sick, Dad?" I said.

He looked up at me, almost like he didn't recognize me. "I got fired, Petey."

I stood there staring at him. I couldn't believe it. "You got fired? Mr. O'Connor fired you?"

Mom came out of the kitchen wiping her hands. "Don't bother Dad right now, Petey," she said.

He waved at her. "It's all right, Meg. I'd just as soon talk."

I still couldn't believe it. "I thought Mr. O'Connor promised you'd always have a job with Allied."

"He did. But he fired me all the same. He called in three of us this morning and let us go. Me, Jack Podolsky the office manager, and Phil Greenberg the chief accountant. He said he was sorry as he could be, but the company was bleeding money and he had to cut somewhere. It was a choice between firing a few executives with the higher salaries or eight or nine people on the shop floor. He said he could get along with fewer management people, but he had to have the workers on the floor to turn out the product. That was it. We went back to our offices, cleaned out our desks, and an hour later we were gone. Just like that. Twenty-two years there, and in an hour it was all over." He shook his head, set the beer bottle on the arm of the chair, and rubbed his eyes with his hands. I thought for a minute he was going to cry. But he didn't. Instead he took a swig of beer. "I stood in front of O'Connor's desk with Jack and Phil, saying to myself, 'This isn't happening, I'm not hearing this.'" He shook his head again. "But it was happening. The truth is, Petey, I should have seen it coming. I've known for a couple of years that the company was in trouble. I just didn't want to see how bad it was. That's human nature for you—you always assume that lightning will strike the other fellow."

Mom slid her hip down on the arm of Dad's chair. "Victor, don't worry. You'll find something right away. You're a good, experienced businessman. You'll get a job."

"Well," he said, "I hope so."

I'd never seen Dad so down, like all the life had been sucked out of him. He wasn't like Dad anymore. "Maybe Mr. O'Connor will change his mind, Dad."

"Yes, you hope that he'll find he can't get along without you. But it isn't realistic. He'll promote somebody off the shop floor to do my job for half the money. The guy won't do as good a job as I would, but O'Connor will live with it. Who knows, the whole company may go under, anyway. Maybe I'm better off getting out now. Well, I'll find a job."

But he didn't find a job. He spent a few days with Gramps out at the farm, helping him plant the corn, the way he'd done when he'd been a boy. The bank still hadn't foreclosed: the government had put through a program to help farmers pay off their debts. Gramps hadn't got into it, but the bank said they'd wait; they'd rather do that than take over the farm. When Dad came back he had a little more spirit in him. He began making phone calls and lining up interviews. Doing something made him feel more hopeful, he said. "Something's bound to turn up. I'm still young. My record's good."

But nothing turned up. This company wasn't hiring, that company might have an opening in a couple of months, the other company was impressed with his record and would keep him in mind. That was the way it went. He always had something in front of him to give him hope—a company that said it expected to be hiring somebody soon, a company he heard about that was looking for a man with just his experience. But the days went by and he was still out of work.

One day when I came in after school, he was sitting in his chair, the newspaper job-ads lying on the floor beside him. He was staring out the window at the auto supply store, and he didn't turn his head when I came in. "Dad," I said.

He turned. "Hello, Petey."

"Dad, why can't you get a job from Uncle Mort?"

He turned his head again to look out the window. His whole face was sad. "Mort's the only reason we'll have something to eat for supper tonight."

I was shocked. "You mean we're so broke we can't afford food?"

Finally he stopped staring out the window and looked at me. "That's right, Petey. All we've got is Ruth's wages. Mort doesn't have a job for me or anyone else at Rayfield Chrome. He said there wasn't any point in putting me on the payroll so I could come in every day and sharpen pencils. We agreed that it would be better for me to go on looking for a job, and in the meanwhile he'd send us money to tide us over. It isn't much, but between that and what Ruth brings in we can pay the rent and buy food. I figured all along that when we sold the house we'd get straightened out financially, but it's the same story there—nobody's buying houses."

All at once I saw that I couldn't take my allowance anymore. In fact, I ought to try to get an after-school job. "Dad, you don't have to give me an allowance anymore."

"I appreciate that, Petey. But I guess we can manage a quarter a week."

"No, you don't have to."

He gave me a little smile. "Petey, you're not going to get anything else. No treats, no movies, no new clothes for a while. I want you to have a little something in your pocket when the other kids go to the soda shop. Let me salvage at least that much pride."

I decided I would take the quarter if he remembered to give it to me. But I wouldn't ask for it on Saturday morning the way I always did. I had a little money I'd saved towards a new Elgin watch. I'd use that first. I'd worry about the watch when I got a job and was earning some money.

But when I went out looking for a job I found out there weren't any. First I went around to Mr. Santini at the grocery store. "I could make deliveries for you," I said.

He laughed. "Petey, I got grown men coming in here almost every day who'll make deliveries for nothing, just for the tips. A nickel or a dime for climbing three or four flights of stairs with a box of groceries."

It was the same story at other stores: there were hundreds of kids around the neighborhood looking for jobs, and generally somebody had got there ahead of me. Sometimes I'd get lucky, happen along when the regular boy was sick or something, and I'd earn a quarter for sweeping, unpacking crates of oranges, shelving cans of vegetables. I'd work as hard and as fast as I could, trying to impress the store owner, but in a day or two the regular boy would be back, and I'd be out of a job. I was beginning to learn how Dad was feeling—my pride was hurt that a lot of kids had jobs and I couldn't get one.

It was funny about that, for it was the same way with the other kids at school. When Dad got fired I happened to tell Eddie Driscoll. Word got around school pretty quick. Of course I wasn't the only kid in school whose dad was out of work—that was pretty common. But in our gang I was the only one. At first I didn't notice anything, but the problem came up pretty quick. Back when Dad still had a job, whenever I needed money for something special I'd ask him for it. Say everybody was going to a certain movie on Saturday, or over to the roller skating rink, or out to a Cubs game, I'd ask him for 50 cents or a dollar—whatever it was going to cost. Now I couldn't ask him for money—wouldn't ask him—even if I thought he might give it to me.

And the first time somebody said, "Hey, who wants to go to the roller rink on Saturday?" I said I couldn't, Mom was taking me shopping for new pants. The next time they were all going to see *Scarface* and the new Mickey Mouse cartoon at the Saturday matinee. I told them the pants didn't fit right, and we had to take them back.

But I saw that I couldn't go on making up excuses forever; I would have to tell the truth sometime. So the next time it came up about the Saturday matinee, I said, "I can't. We can't afford it anymore since Dad lost his job." Eddie Driscoll was there, and Johnny Bright and some of the others. They all stared at me like I'd suddenly grown an elephant's trunk. "You can't even afford to go to the movies?" Eddie said.

Suddenly I didn't want to explain anything to anybody—about Uncle Mort supporting us and all. "He'd give me some money if I asked him, but I don't want to ask him."

"That's tough," Eddie said.

I shrugged. I didn't want them feeling sorry for me, either. "A lot of people are pulling in their reins these days," I said.

After that things began to change. It wasn't that they stopped speaking to me or anything. But I began to notice when I came up to two or three of them that they'd suddenly stop talking. A couple of days later I'd hear one of them say something about a movie they'd just seen or the scary ride they'd gone on at the amusement park. They were beginning to leave me out of things. It wasn't just the things that cost money, either, for I found out that a couple of times they'd gone over to Johnny Bright's house to play cards in his garage and hadn't told me. I was out of my old gang because we were poor. It was that simple.

It was a funny thing: it wasn't my fault that we were poor, it wasn't even Dad's fault. Our family hadn't changed—Mom and Ruth and Dad and me—we were all the same people we'd always been. But even so, I felt like it was my fault. I felt like I wasn't as good as the others somehow. Why would having money or not having money make you feel you weren't as good as other people? I couldn't answer that question, but it did.

After a while I got kind of sore about it. If Eddie or Johnny or somebody did happen to ask me to do something with them, I'd say I couldn't. I didn't want any favors from them, not when they'd cut me out of the gang.

Suddenly I wanted to see Charlie Henrich again. At least he would be one guy who I was as good as. Charlie and I were down around the same level now.

The next Saturday morning off I went to Shacktown. I didn't tell anybody where I was going, but I'd have told them the truth if they'd asked. I guess they figured I was looking for a job. I walked through the slums, past the shut-up factories until I was standing at the edge of the shacktown. I was a little nervous about running into Joey again, or somebody else who might cause me trouble, but I looked more like I belonged there than I had the time before. My shoes were old and scuffed, and there were holes in the bottoms of them; I'd put pieces of cardboard inside them so I wouldn't wear holes in my socks. I'd outgrown my windbreaker, and one of the buttons was different from the others, for I'd lost the original one and Mom hadn't been able to find one to match in her sewing basket. Mom had let the legs of my pants down so they were long enough, but they were old and faded, and so was my shirt. I figured I fit in with Shacktown pretty well.

It looked just the same: same shacks, same weeds growing here and there, same thrown-away people. It was a place without time—didn't get any better, didn't get any worse.

I peered around, looking for Charlie. I didn't see him, nor Joey either. I walked in among the shacks, trying to remember where Charlie's shack was. The people standing around didn't pay much attention to me—gave me a glance and looked away again. Finally I came to a shack that looked like Charlie's. "Hey, Charlie," I called. There was no answer. I stuck my head around the rug. The picture of Gabby Hartnet was still on the wall. But nobody was at home.

I pulled my head out and turned around, feeling disappointed. I'd been looking forward to telling him all the things that had happened. I stood there looking around hoping I might spot him. And then I saw a tall, thin guy with red hair coming towards me. It was Joey. I thought of making a run for it, but I didn't want to be yellow. Besides, I hadn't got anything on me worth stealing. I stood there, my heart thumping.

He came up. "What're you messin' around with that shack for?"

"Nothing. I was looking for my friend."

"Yeah? What friend?"

"Charlie Henrich. He said to meet him here, but he isn't home."

"Home?" he said. "Nice looking home, ain't it?"

"Have you seen him around?"

He squinted at me. "Who's askin'?"

"I'm an old friend. We were in the—" Then I shut my mouth.

"Aha. The kid with the watch. I guess by now your folks got you another one. Let's see it."

I backed up a step. I wished now I hadn't been worried about being yellow and had run for it. "They didn't give me a new one. They don't know I lost it."

"We'll see about that." He lunged for me. I jumped back and banged up against the side of Charlie's shack. He shot out his arm and grabbed the front of my windbreaker. I was scared, but I was mad too. I slammed my fist down on his hand where he'd got hold of my shirt. He grabbed hold of my shoulder and started to twist me around. I swung my fist as hard as I could and caught him on the side of his head. "You little rat," he shouted. He balled up his fist and pulled it back.

Then I heard Charlie shout, "Let him go, Joey."

Joey spun his head around. Charlie was standing by the corner of the shack, holding a piece of two-by-four. He'd grown since I'd last seen him. He looked older, and tougher, somehow. "Let go of him, Joey." He cocked the two-by-four over his shoulder.

Joey let go of my shirt. "The little rat slugged me."

"You started it," I said.

Joey looked at me, then back at Charlie. Finally he decided he couldn't take on the two of us, especially as Charlie had the two-by-four. "Seein' as he's a friend of yours," he said and walked away, rubbing the side of his head where I'd slugged him.

We went into Charlie's shack and sat on his bed, and I told him the whole story—about moving to a little apartment, Dad losing his job, us going broke, and me getting cut out of my old gang.

"At least your dad didn't kill himself," he said. "Is he going to jail?"

"No, nothing like that. He didn't do anything wrong. His company was going broke and they had to lay some people off.

"My dad didn't do anything wrong, either."

I wasn't sure that I believed that anymore. The more I heard about the things that had gone on, the more I realized that an awful lot of people had been cheating one way or another. But I didn't say that. "It's just killing Dad that he can't get a job. It's making him feel awful. He's gotten a few temporary jobs, but he can't get anything regular."

"Well, I'm sorry," he said. "I just hope you don't end up out here."

"I don't guess we will," I said. I figured Uncle Mort would never let that happen to us.

"I hope not," he said.

Suddenly I realized I'd made a mistake thinking that Charlie would see me as on his level. I had a warm apartment to live in, regular meals, a chance to take a hot bath; so far as he was concerned, I wasn't much worse off than I'd been before. So what if I had to share a room? "I just wish Dad could get a job."

"Hey," Charlie said suddenly. "Know what, Petey? I think I got a job."

"Really? What kind of a job?"

"I don't know for sure. Some guy is coming out here pretty soon who's got a lot of jobs. Three dollars a day and meals."

"What doing?"

"I don't know exactly. Working in some factory somewhere. There's a whole bunch of us going from here."

The whole thing sounded strange to me. How come there would be a whole lot of jobs for people from Shacktown when Dad couldn't get a job? "What factory? How come there are a lot of jobs?"

Suddenly Charlie looked worried. "Maybe I shouldn't

have said anything. You won't tell anybody, will you, Petey?"

"I don't get it, Charlie."

"Promise you won't tell anyone?"

"Okay, I won't tell."

"They're going on strike in this factory. We're going to get their jobs."

I didn't mean to gasp, but I did. "You're going to be a strike-breaker? A scab? You're going to cross a picket line?"

He looked me hard in the face. "Sure I would. Why not? What good have unions ever done me?"

He was right. What good had anybody ever done him? Still, it shocked me that he'd scab. I tried to think of what Steve would have said. "Charlie, the workers have to stick together. You can't let the bosses play you off against each other.

He gave me a disgusted look. "What's the use of that malarkey when you live in a shack and figure you're lucky if you get a piece of fatback with your beans?"

"Charlie, once they settle the strike they'll fire all you guys and hire back the old workers. You'll be right back in Shacktown in a couple of weeks."

"So what? In the meantime I'll earn a few bucks, and get myself three squares a day. You're living in a house and eating regular. What right have you got to tell me I shouldn't go to work in that place?"

He was right. I didn't have any business telling him he shouldn't take the chance to eat well for a few days. I took a deep breath. I'd come out to Shacktown looking for somebody I could tell my troubles to, and I'd ended up in an argument. "Okay, Charlie, I guess it's your right to decide."

And it wasn't until I was walking home that it suddenly dawned on me how much I'd come around to Steve's way of looking at things. It had crept up on me bit by bit. It hadn't been any one thing, nothing suddenly sweeping over me. It had been everything slowly piling up—seeing Charlie scavenging in garbage cans the first time, the auction at Gramps's farm, losing the house, Dad sitting home day after day staring out the window, me getting cut out of my gang. Something was wrong somewhere; things had to change.

Chapter 11

The Depression was like one of those ogres in fairy tales, who lives in the dark woods outside of some old peasant village. A big, hairy kind of ogre, with a crooked nose, ripped ears, huge red eyes, teeth like little daggers. Every once in a while it sneaks into the village at night, steals some kid away and eats him raw. Nobody in the village ever sees the ogre, except maybe a glimpse out a window as he flashes by in the moonlight, but they know he's out there, and that sooner or later he's going to pounce again.

The Depression was like that. You couldn't see it or hear it, but it was always there, like that ogre, now pouncing on this one, now pouncing on that one, and you never knew who would be next. It had pounced on Charlie Henrich, pounced on Gramps, pounced on us.

Dad tried to keep his spirits up. He would always say that he had a lead on something that looked good, nothing definite of course, but it had a good chance of coming through. But sometimes, when I came into the living room without warning, I'd catch him slumped in his chair, staring down at the floor—just staring. Then he'd realize I was there and would snap his head up and swing into some cheerful conversation—about how the Cubs were doing or some new program coming out of Washington that might improve things.

In fact, Dad did get a few jobs here and there along the way. One summer, 1934, he worked for a few weeks in an amusement park selling tickets for rides. That ended when the summer was over. He took some kind of a test the school board gave, and signed up as a substitute teacher in accounting, which he knew about, and a few times a month he'd be called in to substitute for a day or two here and there. At Christmastime there was always work in the department stores that needed clerks or gift wrappers; and right after Christmas that year, he got a real job in a factory as a supervisor, filling in for somebody who was really sick. "Would you get the job if he died?" Ruth asked.

"I think so," he said. "But we mustn't hope for that." But the guy got better and Dad was out of work again. Still, it was amazing how much he cheered up when he had a job, any kind of a job, even selling tickets for rides. It wasn't so much the money, it was his self-respect. A man ought to be working, he believed, and it made him feel a whole lot better when he was.

That summer, we finally got another long letter from Steve. He'd been in the longshoreman's strike out in San Francisco. The papers were full of it. A couple of the strikers had got killed. Dad read Steve's letter over dinner.

> . . . The shipowners figured we'd give in pretty quick, but we didn't. By the beginning of July the strike was hurting them, so they decided to bring in strikebreakers. They had 700 cops to protect the scabs, but we fought them off. We fought them with clubs, stones, bare fists. There was blood running in the

streets. A lot of our guys ended up in the hospital. The next day was July 4th and they held off for the holiday. On July 5th they came at us again with hundreds of strikebreakers and 800 cops. They came after us with the clubs and when they couldn't break through, they used tear gas and began to shoot. Two of our guys were killed. We fought them all day until midnight, when the governor sent in 5,000 National Guardsmen to take over the waterfront. A few days later thousands of us paraded up Market Street carrying the coffins of the two men who got killed. The message got across to working people that the bosses would stop at nothing, even killing people, to break a strike. The unions formed a strikers' committee and shut San Francisco down. That scared the bosses—they thought the revolution had come. So both sides agreed to binding arbitration of the longshoremen's grievances by a government committee. Whatever the committee decides, everybody has to accept it. We're pretty sure we're going to get what we want. Everybody knows that if we go back to the old way there will be a revolution for certain.

When Dad got finished reading I shouted, "Yea, Steve!" and Ruth and I clapped our hands.

Mom and Dad looked serious. Mom said, "I wish Steve didn't get himself involved in these things. It's very dangerous."

Dad shook his head. "I never thought I'd see a time in the United States when they'd send the police out to shoot working people. Still, the strikers were taking the law into their own hands. Whether anyone likes it or not, the shipowners have a legal right to employ whoever they want."

"Dad," Ruth cried, "you can't be on the side of the shipowners."

He shook his head again. "No, I'm not on their side, Ruth. I don't like what they've been doing any more than you do. But I will tell you, despite everything we've gone through, I still have faith in capitalism. You've got to let the system work without too much interference from government. It worked before, and it'll work again. Yes, I can see that this arbitration idea they're going to try with the longshoremen's union was probably necessary in this case. But you don't want the government always stepping in to set wages and hours. The next thing you know, the government will be running industry altogether. It won't work. You've got to let the natural laws of supply and demand operate."

"But Dad, they brought in cops," I said. "That's government interference, isn't it?"

"The strikers were breaking the law. The owners had the legal right to bring the strikebreakers in."

"Maybe they shouldn't have a legal right," Ruth said.

"Maybe not," Dad said. "But until the law is changed, we have to abide by it."

"All right," Mom said, "That's enough talk of politics for one evening. Let's enjoy our dinner."

But Steve was right: a few weeks later the government arbitration board gave the longshoremen most of what they wanted. I was reading the newspapers a whole lot more carefully now and saw it for myself, but we got a letter from Steve about it too. "We won," he said. "The tide is turning in America. The workers are going to get their rights."

But if the tide was turning, it wasn't noticeable to us. Winter came, and then spring, and still Dad hadn't found a job. But Roosevelt's New Deal government was trying. In the spring of 1935 it put through the Works Progress Administration, which everybody called the WPA. The idea was to hire unemployed people to do things like build roads, post offices, bridges, and such, which were needed anyway. Dad said, "I'm against it on principle. The government shouldn't be doing things that private enterprise can do. The government's getting deeper and deeper in debt with these schemes. But I can't see where there's much choice—we can't let children starve because their fathers can't get work." He went down himself to see about a WPA job. All they had was pick-and-shovel jobs. They wanted young men for that, but they put him on the waiting list.

Then, that summer the government put through what they called Social Security. It gave people money for retirement, helped out handicapped and blind people who couldn't work, and did some other things. The papers said it was "historic" and a "landmark" and such. I asked Dad if he thought it was.

"You know, Petey, we've always had the idea in this country that the government ought to stay out of people's way as much as possible. The less government, the better. It was up to people to solve their own problems. But the Depression has changed a lot of people's thinking. They see people with problems they can't solve—no jobs, savings gone down the drain when the banks failed, can't turn to their relatives because they haven't anything either. It was

101

different 50 years ago, when you could always pack and go west and start fresh—California, Oregon, Wyoming. Now there aren't any jobs out there either. And a lot of people are beginning to think that maybe it isn't such a bad idea for the government to step in here and there. They think that maybe the government has a certain responsibility for people who are in trouble through no fault of their own."

"What do you think, Dad?"

He grinned. "I wouldn't mind a little government interference myself right now." He stopped grinning. "But it shouldn't go too far. You don't want government telling you what to do every step of the way."

That summer I turned 14 and could get a real job. It gave me some things to think about. Mom had always said that I was to go to college, like Ruth, and she still wanted me to. If I studied real hard and got good grades I could probably get a scholarship. I could go someplace in Chicago and live at home. But I wasn't so sure I wanted to anymore. Eddie Driscoll and Johnny Bright would go to college, and so would a lot of the others in my old gang. But how could I go even if I got a scholarship, when I ought to be bringing in some money to help the family out? I even thought about dropping out of school to get a job, but neither Mom nor Dad would hear of it. So I went over to Ruth's cafeteria and begged the guy to take me on as a busboy. Two weeks later he fired some kid for coming in 10 minutes late, so he told Ruth to have me come in the next afternoon. I scrubbed myself up good and went over 15 minutes early. The job was clearing up the tables during the evening rush, five o'clock to seven. I'd done hard work before out on the farm, getting in the hay and such. Being a busboy wasn't so hard. But it was more nerve-wracking, for you had to clear each table the minute the customers got up so somebody else could sit down, and there were only three busboys on the shift—not nearly enough. We were always a couple of tables behind, and Mr. Gilkey was yapping at our heels. "Come on, Williamson, I'm not paying you to stand around picking your nose, let's get a move on," he'd say as I was staggering out to the kitchen trying not to drop a trayful of plates and glasses. Oh, it was the worst kind of work I'd ever done, and my heart always sank when I came in at five o'clock and tied on my apron. But the pay was 25 cents an hour, and a free meal thrown in; and what with working a full shift on Saturday, I was making five bucks a week. I gave Mom four, saved 50 cents in a tin can for new shoes or pants, put a dime aside for a watch, and spent the other half a buck on myself for a movie and a soda on Saturday night. Hard as the work was, it gave me a good feeling to be paying my own way. It made me more of a man. Dad and Mom saw that, and they weren't so quick to tell me what to do as they had been.

So another Christmas with a tiny tree, and one present each for everybody, came and went. And then one day not long after Christmas, I came in from the cafeteria and there was Steve, sitting on the sofa talking with Dad and Mom.

Chapter 12

Steve looked thinner than ever—gaunt, almost. He
hadn't had a haircut for awhile and his blond hair was
down to his collar. He was wearing blue jeans and a blue
work shirt. A brown cloth cap lay on the sofa beside him.
He got up and would have hugged me the way he used
to, but I was too old for hugs now, and we shook hands.
"Are you going to stay home for awhile?" I asked him.

"I'll only be in Chicago for a few days," he said. "I was
telling your dad, I've been working on some strike
committees for the C.I.O. Did you know I was out in
Akron this spring when they struck the rubber plants?"

The strike at the Goodyear plant had been in all the
papers. I was glad I'd kept up with it. "The first sit-down
strike."

"Oh, it was terrific," Steve said. "It was totally
spontaneous. Nobody could say it was stirred up by the
unions or the Communists. The workers on the shop
floor did it themselves. They just took the factory over.
Admittedly, John L. Lewis had given a hot speech out
there just a few days before, but the workers did it
themselves. In the end Goodyear gave in."

Dad was listening carefully. "Steve, I have to hand it

to you. You've stuck to your guns. I don't agree with everything you're doing, but it takes guts. I don't have to tell you it's risky. You could get your head knocked in."

"Dad," I said, "even you agree they shouldn't tear gas strikers."

"Look, Petey," Dad said, "you take some fellow who's spent his life building up a company, has a plant worth a few million dollars. He's not going to sit on his hands when the workers try to take over. He'll bring in the police if he can, and if he can't, he'll hire his own security force to break the picket line. Then there's violence and people get hurt. There were two killed in the longshoremen's strike, two killed when they struck the Electric Auto-Lite Company in Toledo, some more killed in Milwaukee during the truckers' strike. Not just union men but people on both sides. You talk about strikers' rights; but the Constitution is pretty strong about people being able to do what they want with their own property."

Steve smiled. "I'm not going to comment, Uncle Vic."

Dad decided to drop the subject. "So where are you off to now, Steve?"

"I'm going up to Flint, Michigan. I'm going to work on the sit-down strike at GM's Fisher Body plant. It's a great situation. You've got 15 hundred men sitting down inside the plant. They elected their own mayor, got their own barber shop, a post office. Organized sports. They're going to beat General Motors."

"We'll see," Dad said. "GM is pretty resourceful."

"I've got to go," Steve said. He picked up his cap and

105

stood. "Uncle Vic, did Pop tell you they're trying to organize Rayfield Chrome?"

Dad turned his head to look out the window. "He didn't tell me, Steve. But I heard it." He went on looking out the window at the auto supply store.

"What do you think, Uncle Vic?"

Dad turned back to Steve. "It's going to be a mess if it happens. I know Mort. He won't compromise. He won't give an inch."

"I know," Steve said. "That's one reason why I came over tonight. He won't listen to me, he won't listen to Ma. He might listen to you. Maybe you can talk some sense into him. A lot of times if you throw the strikers a bone they'll settle. Half of the work union organizers do is keeping the members from settling too easily."

Dad nodded. "I understand that. But making Mort understand that is another thing."

"Please try," Steve said. Then he left.

I was always sorry to see Steve go, but this time I felt something more. I envied him. He was going off to be involved with something important, something that might change the United States, somehow. I wanted to go there too. But I couldn't—not until I was older. I'd have to wait.

Three days later there was a little story in the paper about Uncle Mort's company. It was only a small story on page 17, but when I saw it I knew that the ogre had pounced once more. They were going to vote on striking Rayfield Chrome. "Management refuses to negotiate with the union," the newspaper story said. Management, I

106

knew, was Uncle Mort. He wasn't going to give an inch.

That night, when I was working at the cafeteria, Dad went over to see Uncle Mort. He came home around eight o'clock, looking grim. "He's going to fight all the way. He says he doesn't want to bring in scabs, but he will if he has to. 'At least meet with the union leaders, Mort,' I said, but he won't. 'I'm not going to have a bunch of Commies tell me how to run my factory,' he says."

Two days later the workers went out on strike. They formed a picket line in front of the plant. "Dad, is he going to bring in scabs?"

"He'll do whatever he thinks he has to, to beat the union."

I knew what I was going to do, for I knew where there were a lot of people who were willing to scab. And on Sunday I set off for the shacktown. By this time I was looking even more like the thrown-away people: Mom had patched my shirt, patched my pants, put elbow patches on my windbreaker. I'd finally bought myself a pair of cheap new shoes for a dollar out of my savings, but they were already getting shabby.

At the shacktown nobody paid any attention to me. I found Charlie in his shack, sitting in the chair with half the cane seat out of it, huddled close to the fire in the lard can. Beside the stove sat a bucket of coal. Charlie was eating a big fried-egg sandwich on a roll, dripping with ketchup and drinking from a quart bottle of cream soda. "Hey, Petey," he said.

I ducked through the carpet door and went in. "Where'd you get the bucket of coal?"

107

"I got some money," he said.

"You got a job?"

He looked away. Then he looked back at me. "Yeah, I got a job."

He didn't have to tell me. "Scabbing," I said.

"What's it to you? It isn't any of your business what I do. You want me to sit around here freezing to death?"

"I didn't say anything, Charlie. I just asked if you had a job."

"Well don't start bawling me out."

"I'm not going to," I said. I stood there trying to think of how Steve would handle it. "Nobody wants you to freeze to death. I don't blame you for scabbing. I'd do the same if I was cold and hungry. I just wish there was some way you could earn some money without scabbing."

"Ha," he said. "Don't you think I wish it too?"

I sat down on the bed. "How'd it work out last time?"

He shrugged. "Just the way you figured. The strike lasted for 10 days. Then they took strikers back and let us go. But it was 10 days of easy living—plenty of coffee and rolls for breakfast, a good hot lunch every day."

"You getting a lot of that kind of work?"

He shrugged again. "I've had two or three the past couple of months. I keep hoping that one of them'll turn into a regular job, but they won't. Once the strikers come back, they don't want any of the scabs around. They beat the heck out of a couple of our guys who tried to keep the jobs."

"That's not surprising," I said. "Where's this new job?"

"It hasn't started yet. They guess it'll happen in a

108

couple of days. They spread a few dollars around to make sure we'd be ready when they want us."

"What kind of work is it?"

"I forget. It doesn't make any difference. They send around some trucks and take you there."

"You can't even remember where you're going to work?"

"I wrote it down." He reached into his shirt pocket and took out a slip of paper. "Some place called Rayfield Chrome."

I got out of there as soon as I could and walked home fast. What was I going to do? The trouble was, I liked Uncle Mort. He was blustery and all that, but any time Steve took me out to Wrigley Field to see the Cubs Uncle Mort gave me a buck for hot dogs and soda. Besides, he'd been helping to support us ever since Dad had got fired.

But I wasn't on his side. Once upon a time, long, long ago, I'd been the child of one of the bosses and had been able to see both sides of the argument. But I wasn't that person now, any more than I was the person who'd had *Chicken Little* read to him. I was a worker getting paid 25 cents an hour to clean up tables from other people's dinners and get yapped at regular if I stopped moving for 10 seconds to scratch myself. I couldn't side with Uncle Mort against the workers: that'd be siding against myself.

I wished I could talk with Steve about it. I tried to think if there was some way to call him, but I figured he was inside the Fisher Body plant in Flint and there wouldn't be any way to call. In the end I decided not to say anything to anyone. Maybe it wouldn't happen.

109

Three days later, when I came home from the cafeteria, Mom and Dad were putting their hats and coats on. "Leave your jacket on," Dad said. "We're going over to Uncle Mort's."

I looked at my parents. "What's the matter?"

"Steve's hurt," Mom said. "We've got to see if we can do anything for Mort and Mae."

"Hurt? Hurt bad? What happened?"

"He'll be all right," Dad said. "He'll have to take it easy for a while."

"What happened? Where's Ruth?"

"She's out with that fellow from night school," Mom said.

"Let's go," Dad said. "We'll tell you about it on the way."

I sat between them on the streetcar. "You must have read about it, Petey," Dad said. "It was all over the papers. General Motors was trying to get the strikers out of Fisher Body. They shut off the heat and padlocked the gates so nobody could send in food. The workers broke open the locks. Management brought the Flint police in with tear gas. The workers fought back and the cops began to shoot."

I knew this because I'd followed it pretty close in the papers. "They shot Steve?"

"He got hit. Nobody got killed, but a bunch were wounded. You know Steve, Petey. He was bound to be right in the middle of it. He got hit twice."

I sat there feeling scared and sick to my stomach.

What if Steve had got killed? What if we were going to a
funeral home to see Steve lying in a coffin? "Is he
unconscious, Dad?"

"No, I don't think so. He might be asleep when we get
there, though."

But he wasn't. He was sitting on the sofa in the living
room in his pajamas, propped up with a couple of
pillows, eating a piece of cake. He had a bandage around
his head and a cast on his shoulder that went halfway
down his arm, so that his pajama top was draped around
him. "Hello everybody," he shouted, grinning. "Come to
see the wounded soldier?"

Just then Uncle Mort and Aunt Mae came in. Aunt
Mae was carrying a tray with the coffee things and cake
on it.

Dad patted Steve on his good shoulder. "You seem to
be in pretty good spirits, Steve."

"Why wouldn't I be? We're going to win this thing.
They threw cops at us, tear gas, but we fought them off.
We threw anything we could find. Bottles, stones, metal
car parts. They quit and we kept the plant."

I glanced at Uncle Mort. He was gloomily drinking
coffee and eating a piece of cake. He didn't say anything.

"You'd think they'd learn," Steve said. "Every time
some worker gets gunned down the rest get more
determined to fight." He looked at his father. "Sometimes
all you have to do with workers is to give way on a few
small points."

Uncle Mort scowled. "I'm not going to have a bunch

111

of Commies tell me how to run my business." He looked at Dad. "They're probably going to go out on strike tomorrow. I can't believe it. I never thought my people would turn against me. After everything I've done for them. I haven't taken a cent of profit out of that place for two years. I could have closed it down, but I didn't, I kept it going so my people would have jobs. Now that things have picked up a little and I have a chance to make up for the bad years, they're going on strike. It isn't the money that hurts so much, it's the loyalty. I've tried to be the best employer I could. I didn't come out of some business college. I know what it's like to be on the shop floor. I know most of my people by name, and if I knew a man was in trouble, had a lot of kids or a sick wife, I'd do my best to keep him. And now they strike me."

It was strange to see Uncle Mort hurt and downhearted, like a little kid whose ball of ice cream has fallen out off the cone into the dirt. Dad listened closely, but he didn't say much. I figured he didn't agree with everything Uncle Mort was saying, but didn't want to argue about it right then.

There was a whole lot I wanted to talk to Steve about, but I couldn't with Uncle Mort there. But the next night I went right to the Rayfields' house from the cafeteria. Uncle Mort was still at the factory, and Aunt Mae was out at some charity, so I had Steve to myself. He was sprawled out on the living-room sofa in his pajamas, reading. "I'm glad you came, Petey. I was getting bored. I'm not used to sitting around like this anymore."

I sat down in Uncle Mort's easy chair. "How long are you going to be laid up?"

He shrugged. "So far as the head goes, it's only a scratch. It'll heal in a week. The shoulder cast will have to stay on for a month. I'm too restless to sit around that long. I'm going back soon."

"Were you scared when they started to shoot?"

"I was too busy to think about it. I guess I was scared. But mostly excited. It was exhilarating. I didn't even notice when I got hit in the shoulder. Three or four of us were pushing a huge crate against a window for a barricade, and I was sweating and straining so hard I didn't notice. When I got hit in the head it was just like they say—I saw fireworks. The next thing I knew somebody was bending over me asking me if I was dead."

"Did you think you were going to die?"

"No. I figured if you didn't die right off when you got hit in the head, you weren't going to."

"You must hate cops," I said.

He shook his head. "No, I don't. A lot of the men do, but I don't. They were just following orders. A lot of them are on our side at heart anyway. They have brothers, relatives, who're on the shop floor."

"But they were shooting at you."

"Well, legally GM had a right to get us out of there, and if we were resisting the cops, they had a right to shoot. But there's another way of looking at it. The only thing some of these people like Pop, the executives at GM, the bosses, can see are property rights. What about people's rights? I mean the right to a decent job with a wage you can feed your kids on? Enough so you can buy them a new pair of shoes when they need them, go to the doctor when they're sick. Did you know that there are millions of Americans who can't afford to go to the doctor when they're sick? I've seen kids barefoot in the street because their folks can't afford to buy them shoes."

"Steve, I have to tell you something." I took a deep breath. "Your Pop is planning to bring in scabs if his workers go out."

He sat there, staring at me. Then he said, "Where'd you get that?"

"Remember that kid I know who's living over in Shacktown? I was over there a little while ago. He said somebody came over to line up strikebreakers for Rayfield Chrome."

"Are you sure he said it was Rayfield?"

"Positive. He had it written down on a scrap of paper. I saw it."

Steve hung his head down. He sat there for a long while staring at the floor. Finally he raised his head up. "Petey, can you take me out there? I want to talk to that kid."

Chapter 13

The workers struck Rayfield Chrome two days later. There was a story about it in the paper. The main issue, the story said, was unionization. The workers wanted the C.I.O. to represent them in negotiations over pay and hours. "Management, however, has said it will not deal with the union and appears unwilling to bend on this issue."

"What's he going to do, Dad?" I said that night as we all sat around the living room, discussing it.

"You know Mort. He'll fight."

"What if he brings in scabs?"

"I sincerely hope he won't. This rash of strikes we've had over the past few months has taught the unions that they can win if they stand firm. There could be violence."

I'd been following things pretty closely now, and I knew about all of this. In 1935 the government had passed the Wagner Act, which gave the workers the right to unionize, to strike, to picket.

"The whole thing is perfectly awful," Mom said. "Poor Mort. He's worked so hard to keep the plant going and now this." He was her brother; she was bound to take his side.

But I knew that Uncle Mort was planning to bring in scabs. "Dad, if you knew that Uncle Mort was bringing in scabs, would you try to stop him?"

"Petey," Mom said, "I wish you wouldn't use that word."

"Why not?"

"It's not a nice word."

"The girls at the cafeteria say it all the time," Ruth said.

"Those girls say a lot of things I hope you don't say," Mom replied.

Dad was ignoring this, and frowning down into his hands, the way he did. "Well, let's hope it doesn't come to strikebreakers. Let's hope Mort's able to work things out somehow. Because I'll tell you all something." He looked at me and then Ruth and then back at me again. "If he does, he's bound to ask me to go in and supervise them. And what with everything he's done for us, I'd have to say yes."

There was a dead silence. Ruth and I looked at each other, and then back to Dad. I was shocked and so was Ruth. But there wasn't anything either of us could say.

Steve and I went out to Shacktown the next afternoon. He picked me up in his '31 Oldsmobile. It didn't look so pretty anymore. It had over 100,000 miles on it, there were dents all over the place, the rear window was cracked, and there was a big burn hole in the back seat. "I was hauling a bunch of grape pickers out to a picket line and somebody dropped a cigarette butt down there."

We drove out, parked a few blocks from the shacktown and walked over. Steve stood at the edge, looking around at the shacks, the people clustered around the oil drums.

"Pretty bad, isn't it, Steve?"

"I've seen worse. Some of those migrant workers out there in California don't even have shacks. They're living in tents or sleeping on the ground."

We walked over to Charlie's shack. A few people stared at us, but nobody said anything. I stuck my head around the carpet. Charlie was lying on the bed huddled up in a blanket. We went in. "Charlie, this is my cousin Steve."

Charlie looked at Steve, but he didn't say anything.

"Charlie, Petey told me all about you. He said you maybe could use a good meal. Let's go someplace warm and get something to eat."

Charlie looked at me. "Is he kidding?"

"No," I said.

We went to a place Charlie knew about, a beat-up diner a couple of blocks away, the wood tables scratched and marked with cigarette burns, the cloth of the seats torn. We sat in a booth eating hamburgers and French fries and drinking coffee. I could see that Steve had a lot of practice getting people to talk—asking casual questions, like he didn't mean much by them. It bothered me a little, for he *did* mean something by them, but I didn't want to cross up Steve.

So Charlie told Steve about his dad having to shoot himself twice to make sure he was dead, about living in Shacktown, and begging for a living. He got through one hamburger and Steve bought him another. Then Steve said, "Petey says you've got a job coming up."

"They come up sometimes. You never can tell. It depends on if there's a strike at this place. See, if the workers go out —" Finally he realized that he was talking too much. "I better not say anything about it."

"Petey said it was Rayfield Chrome where you might be working."

Suddenly Charlie seemed to crouch in on himself and get smaller. He darted his eyes around the diner here and there. "I never said that. Petey got it wrong."

"I heard the workers at Rayfield are already out," Steve said. "There should be jobs for you guys."

Charlie was still hunched in on himself. "I don't know anything about it," he said. He started cramming the hamburger in his mouth before anybody took it away.

"Charlie, my pop owns Rayfield Chrome."

Charlie looked as if somebody was about to hit him. His mouth fell open and his eyes blinked. "I didn't do anything," he said. "This guy came out and said he'd give anybody who wanted to work new shoes, meals, and five bucks a day. What did I do wrong? Why shouldn't I?"

Steve laughed. "Charlie, don't panic. You've got a perfect right to take the job. But I think you ought to warn the guys that there's likely to be fighting. The workers at Rayfield aren't going to just stand there and let

118

you guys in." He shrugged. "It's no skin off my nose. Who wants a piece of pie?"

Charlie was scared and wanted to get out of there, but the pie was too tempting for him. He ordered blueberry pie and ice cream, and while he was waiting, Steve said, "Who usually takes you over to these places?"

Charlie darted his eyes around the room again. "Just some guys. They come in old army trucks."

"What kind of guns do they carry? Just sidearms? Or shotguns too?"

Charlie gazed around the room some more. "I wish they'd bring the pie."

Steve laughed again. "All right, Charlie. I'll lay off."

The third day of the strike Steve came over to talk to Dad. "Uncle Vic, he's going to bring in scabs. At first he was sure he could talk the older men around. He's had some of them in the shop for 20 years, knows their families, has a party for their kids at Christmas. He called them in one at a time to talk to them. They shuffled their feet and looked down at their shoes, but they wouldn't back down. Said, 'You always been a good boss, Mr. Rayfield, but the fellas voted and I guess I got to do it.' He was hurt, and now he's sore as a hornet. He won't listen to me. I thought you might be able to reason with him."

"You sure about the strikebreakers?"

"Yes," Steve said. He didn't look at me.

"I told him about it, Dad," I said. "I got it from Charlie Henrich. The guys out at the shacktown get hired to scab sometimes."

Steve nodded. "They'll have goons riding shotgun on the trucks. They'll be armed. I've seen it twice now, once in San Francisco, and then up at Flint." He touched the cast on his shoulder. "I know what happens. People lose their tempers and the whole thing goes off like a bomb."

Dad sat there thinking. Finally he said, "Steve, are you aware that if Mort brings in strikebreakers he's almost certain to ask me to go in and supervise?"

Steve frowned. "I didn't think of that." He looked at Dad. "Would you do it, Uncle Vic?"

I hated the idea that Dad might look bad to Steve. I hoped that he could come up with a good explanation.

"Steve," Dad said, putting his hands behind his head, "I've been out of work for a long time. Picked up something here and there, but not much. Mort's been feeding my family. That hurts, not being able to provide for your own wife and children. I mean it *hurts*. I'll tell you the truth, some days I've skipped shaving because I didn't want to look at my own face in the mirror."

"Victor, we've never blamed you," Mom said. "We know it isn't your fault."

Dad waved his hand. "Oh yes, I know that. I know that. It's the fault of the world situation, the business cycle, the stock market speculators, the money men, the war. Who knows? I don't, surely. But I still haven't lost faith in the capitalist system—free enterprise, whatever you want to call it. In two or three generations we've gone from a nation of farmers to being the richest and most powerful nation on earth. Capitalism had something to do with that, you can't deny it, Steve."

"Can you really credit it all to capitalism?" Steve said. "What about the blacks sweating in the cotton fields, the immigrants in filthy factories working 10 hours a day for peanuts, ordinary Americans like your own dad almost losing his home after spending his life beating his brains out in the hayfield when it was over 100 degrees? These people were in trouble before the Depression."

Dad nodded. "Sure. Yes. I'll grant you that a lot of people got tromped on pretty hard along the way. I was out in those hayfields myself when I was 12 years old, working until it got too dark to see. But you've got to give capitalism some credit in there, Steve. Men who poured their hard-earned savings into some dream, some idea that would make life easier for people. I know what Mort went through to build his business. For years he put in longer hours than any of the men on the floor."

"Uncle Vic, if it were just some little guy sitting in the patent office with an invention under his arm, or somebody like Pop who really did start out with nothing, it would be one thing. But the system isn't being run by them, it's being run by the big money men, the monopolists like Carnegie, J.P. Morgan, Rockefeller, who'll pay their workers as little as they can and then hire goons to shoot them dead when they object, the way they did at Carnegie's Homestead plant.

"Steve, the system isn't perfect. It won't ever be. Nothing on earth ever is. But it's made us the most prosperous nation on earth."

"Prosperous? Look at Charlie Henrich, living in a shack and going hungry half the time. Look at Gramps, sweating bullets he'll be tossed off the farm where he was born and raised and buried his wife. Prosperity? With millions out of work? I don't buy it, Uncle Vic."

"You won't get any argument from me on that, Steve," Dad said. "There are things that have to be fixed. I know that as well as anybody. It may be that Roosevelt's right with some of these New Deal schemes: Social Security. The Wagner Act. Some of these agencies for keeping a sharper watch on the banks, the stock brokers, the sweat shops. I can go along with the government taking a bigger hand in things. But you don't throw the baby out with the bath water." He put his hands behind his head again and looked out the window at the auto supply store. "Then there's this: Are we happier in the United States with our automobiles, our movies, our refrigerators, and all the rest of it than those people out in Asia living in thatched huts and working the rice paddies? Are we happier than those tribesmen in Africa with their herds of cattle? I can't answer that question, and right now I'm not going to try."

He leaned forward again, to look Steve in the face. "But I'll answer the question you asked in the first place, Steve. How do I feel about going into Rayfield Chrome with the strikebreakers? In my heart, I don't like it. My instincts go against it. But I'm going to do it because of what I owe Mort. It's no different from what I did when they were auctioning off Gramps's farm. That auction was legal and we had no right to interfere with it. But I wasn't going to sit still and see an old man thrown off a place where he'd spent his life. Same with Mort. He was there when I needed him. Now he needs me and I'll be there for him."

Nobody said anything for a minute. We sat, each of us thinking. Then Steve said, "Uncle Vic, at least we agree on one thing—human values over property." He took a breath. "Okay. Will you try to talk some sense into Pop?"

Dad gave a little smile. "I can try, Steve. But I wouldn't want to bet a whole lot of money on it."

We sat in the Rayfield's living room, all of us. Aunt Mae brought coffee and slices of lemon cake with thick white icing—you couldn't go into that house without being fed. "Well, Victor," said Uncle Mort, "has Steve turned you into a Socialist?"

Dad smiled. "Not yet, Mort. You know that basically I agree with you about most of these things. You have to give Steve a lot of credit for putting himself on the line for his beliefs and you can be proud of him for that. But he's young, he's idealistic, he doesn't know as much about the world as we do. Nonetheless, he's right about one thing—if you bring in strikebreakers somebody's going to get hurt."

Uncle Mort picked up his coffee cup and blew on it. Then he put the cup down. "I've got a perfect right to hire anyone I want. If my people don't want to work for my money, I'll find some who do."

"Mort," Dad said, "If you try to ram those strikebreakers through the picket line, you're asking for trouble. The pickets aren't going to stand there and cheer while the trucks go through. They'll fight. Men are going to get hurt. You might get lucky, it might not happen, but you're taking a big chance."

Uncle Mort shook his head firmly. "Then it'll be the fault of the strikers, not mine. If the strikers choose to break the law, it's their doing, not mine."

"Suppose someone's killed, Mort?"

Uncle Mort frowned, picked up the cup and bent over it to take a sip. "Well of course I don't want anybody killed. Nobody wants that. But I'm not responsible for what the strikers do."

"Mort, Steve almost got killed in the fight at Fisher Body. If that bullet had gone half an inch to the right we wouldn't be talking about any of this now. It's not just some faint possibility. Mort, do me a favor. Talk to the union guys. As a personal favor to me."

Uncle Mort set his lips and shook his head. "Not a chance," he said, thumping his fist on the arm of the easy chair. "Not one chance, Victor. I spent 25 years working like a dog to build Rayfield Chrome up to what it is. *I* did it, and I did it without the help of these guys from the union who've been sweet-talking my people so they can take my business away from me. Do you think those guys from the C.I.O. really give two cents for my people? All they're interested in is getting power for themselves. I'm the one who's kept that company going, who's paid their salaries, not the C.I.O. How many times do you think I paid a man his wages for weeks when he was sick and couldn't support his family? How many of their kids do you think I've sent away to summer camp? How many of their sons and cousins and nephews do you think I've found jobs for? What about the baseball field I put in so they could play during lunch, what about the Christmas parties with a present for every single kid, what about the Fourth of July picnics, all the beer, hot dogs, and potato salad they could eat? Do you think the union is going to do anything like that for them? Don't you believe it, Victor."

"Pop," Steve said, "Shouldn't the workers have some say-so in how the plant is run?"

"No," Uncle Mort said, thumping his fist on the arm of the chair again. "Somebody has to be boss. Somebody has to make decisions, take responsibility. You can't run a business like a high-school dance committee. These fellas on the shop floor haven't got the faintest idea of what's involved."

And that was the end of it; Uncle Mort wasn't going to budge.

Chapter 14

The next day, after I got out of the cafeteria, I went over to the plant with Steve just to see what was going on. There was a line of pickets, around 50 of them, marching in a circle round and round in front of the steel mesh gate to the factory, carrying signs saying *Rayfield Chrome Unfair, We Demand a Living Wage,* and so forth. They'd got fires going in a couple of tar barrels where they warmed up from time to time, and they'd set up a card table for a coffee urn and boxes of doughnuts to keep themselves cheerful. They were picketing day and night, Steve said, in four-hour shifts. They couldn't leave the place unguarded in case Uncle Mort tried to slip scabs in. They seemed pretty cheerful on the whole, marching and chanting and singing songs like "Joe Hill" and "Union Now."

That was Saturday. On Sunday morning I was woken up early by a noise in the kitchen. I got up and went out in my pajamas. Dad was sitting at the kitchen table, drinking coffee. He was wearing work pants and a blue work shirt. "Where are you going so early, Dad?"

He took a swallow of coffee. "I've got something to do. You go on back to bed."

I noticed a paper bag with the top rolled on the kitchen table. "Are you taking your lunch?"

"No," he said. "It's my razor and stuff. I may be gone overnight. Now you go on back to bed."

"You're going over to Rayfield, aren't you?"

"I didn't say where I was going, did I Petey? If I want you to know, I'll tell you. Now go back to bed." He gulped down the rest of his coffee, put on his coat, picked up the paper bag, and left.

I sat down at the kitchen table to think. He was going to Rayfield, all right. Did that mean the scabs were coming in today? It was getting scary. Suppose there was fighting. Would Dad have to get into it? Did Steve know what was going on? I looked at the kitchen clock: only six-thirty. Not a sound from Mom and Ruth. Was it too early to call Steve? If Dad was on the way to the factory, so was Uncle Mort. I had to call Steve, no matter how early it was. I went out to the living room and phoned. Steve answered. "Did I wake you up?" I said.

"No. I've been up."

"I think Dad's gone over to the plant," I said, speaking as low as I could so as not to wake Mom and Ruth.

"Probably," Steve said. "Something's up. Pop went out a little while ago. He didn't say anything to anybody. He took the Ford station wagon. I figured he'd rather take a chance on it being damaged than the Packard. I woke up when I heard the car go out."

"What're you going to do?"

"I'm going over to Shacktown and talk to the men."

"Take me, Steve," I whispered.

127

There was silence. Finally he said, "It's one thing to take chances myself, Petey. I don't want you getting hurt."

"Please. Please Steve. I'll be careful."

More silence. "All right. But if I tell you to go home, you go. Got it?"

"I promise."

"Be downstairs in 20 minutes."

But I didn't want to hang around for 20 minutes, for fear Mom would get up and stop me. I flung on my old clothes, grabbed a couple of hard rolls out of the refrigerator, and slipped downstairs to the street. It was Sunday: if Mom got up now she'd figure I was still asleep.

In a little while Steve rolled up. I climbed in. "I've got a feeling in my bones there's going to be trouble," he said. "Pop's spoiling for a fight. He's made up his mind he's going to risk somebody getting killed. It isn't really about money anymore, or whether he ought to give the men coffee breaks. It's about who's boss—the union or him."

"I guess he figures it's his plant, he ought to be boss," I said.

Steve gave me a quick look. "Isn't it the workers' plant too? Some of them will spend the best part of their lives there."

Was that a good answer? I didn't know, but I was too nervous to think about it.

Steve drove fast through the empty Sunday morning streets. We parked a couple of blocks away from the shacktown to be safe, and trotted over. There, in the middle of Shacktown were three old army trucks, with dark brown canvas roofs. Behind each truck was a short line of men. "Come on," Steve said. We trotted forward. Now we could see standing at the rear of each truck a man with a clipboard, taking names, as the men from Shacktown climbed one by one into the trucks. Leaning on the trucks, or sitting on the running boards were men in dark blue work pants, dark blue windbreakers, dark blue caps. They were wearing pistol belts, and some of them were carrying shotguns draped over an arm. "Goons," Steve said. "Probably recruited from the mobs."

It was like movies I'd seen of men going to war—the guns, the blue uniforms, the lines of men climbing into canvas-topped trucks. As cold as it was, I could feel sweat on my forehead, and my heart was racing.

Steve ran to the back of the first truck, with me running behind. The tail of men behind the truck looked at us curiously. The man with the clipboard waved at us. "End of the line, you two. No jumping in." I saw Charlie, halfway down the line. His hand was over his face so I wouldn't recognize him, but I did.

Steve cupped his hands around his mouth. "Hey fellows, listen to me for a minute. I want to warn you, the pickets are going to fight. Somebody's going to get hurt. Have some common sense. There's—"

Then one of the goons shouted, "Hey you," and a couple of them began trotting toward us.

"This isn't going to work, Petey," Steve said. "Let's get out of here." We turned and ran back the way we'd come, my breath coming fast. But as soon as the goons saw we were leaving, they stopped chasing us. We flew back to the car and leapt in. "Those goons, those guns," Steve said. "It's going to be a war."

"What're you going to do?"

"Tell Pop about those shotguns. Maybe he'll finally see some sense. I've been through this before, he hasn't."

We reached the factory road and turned in. Men in bunches of two, three, four, were hurrying towards the factory. They were carrying baseball bats, pick handles. "The strikers," Steve said. "They've called everybody in. They're going to fight."

We reached the main gate. The pickets weren't circling anymore but were standing in a solid pack in front of the gate. Steve pulled over, got out, and ran forward towards the men. "Listen, you guys," he shouted. "I've just been out to the shacktown. They're loading up trucks with scabs right now. Three truckloads of them. They've got a bunch of goons with them. They're carrying shotguns. They're not playing games. Please, please, try to stay cool. Don't attack them. Don't throw anything. Don't give them an excuse to start shooting."

"Rayfield," somebody shouted. "We'll fight if we have to. If you don't want anybody hurt, go on in and tell your old man to call off the goons."

"That's what I'm going to do. Please, please stay cool."

He ran back to the car, and we drove around to the rear parking lot. Here there were loading docks. A couple of big trucks sat empty in the lot. We jumped out of the car and ran to a door by the loading docks. Steve jerked a key from his pocket, spilling some change. He unlocked the door, leaving the change laying on the ground. I raced after him. I'd been in the plant a good many times. It had always been filled with the noise of machines, of chain hoists clanking, of pushcarts trundling along, and a smell of acid in the air. It was strange to be there in dead silence, the overhead light bulbs off, only a gray light from outside filtering in through the windows. Our feet rattled on the cement floor.

We went past the vats, the pushcarts loaded with auto headlights and bumpers, up two flights of stairs to the office floor: a receptionist's desk, a couple of sofas, a carpet on the floor, a low table with magazines and last week's newspapers on it. But no people, nobody at the receptionist's desk, nobody waiting for an appointment: just more silence and gray light.

We went through the door behind the desk, and down a hall to a door marked in gold lettering, *Morton Rayfield, President*. Steve pushed the door open. For a moment we stood there, looking in.

Uncle Mort was sitting behind his big mahogany desk, with its pair of telephones, papers, a marble pen set. On the wall behind him was an aerial photograph of the factory, on the floor a carpet. To his left a big window looked out onto the front gate. Distant shouts and cries floated up to us.

Sitting in chairs in front of the desk were two men. One of them was Uncle Mort's vice-president, who I'd met a few times. The other was Dad. They all turned to look at us. Uncle Mort said, "Steve, take Petey home."

I looked at Dad. "Please, I'm not scared." But I was scared. Somebody was going to get hurt; somebody was liable to be killed. Was I really going to see somebody die?

"Pop, we just came from Shacktown," Steve said. "They're on their way over here now. They've got shotguns. Can't you see what you're doing? It's not just your own people. You're risking the lives of those poor guys from the shacks."

Uncle Mort stared at Steve. "If those pickets will let the new workers through, nobody'll get hurt. There's nothing you can do here. Take Petey home."

Steve crossed the room to look out the big window. Then he turned back to Uncle Mort's vice-president. "Can't you talk some sense into him? What harm is there in talking to the unions? Who's it going to hurt?"

The vice-president looked uneasy. "Steve, it's Morton's company. He calls the shots."

Steve looked at Dad. "What about it, Uncle Vic?"

Dad shook his head. "Steve, you know your Pop. He's got his mind made up." Then he looked at me. "All right, Petey, you've seen enough. Go on home."

Suddenly there was a faint roar from below and a squabble of voices. Steve swung back to the window. "Here they come," he said.

We all darted to the big window and stood there in a line, looking out. Down the factory road slowly came three old army trucks. The goons in blue pants and blue windbreakers were standing on the running boards, their arms through the cab windows to hold on. I took a quick look at Uncle Mort. He stared out, his hands jammed deep in his trouser pockets. What was he thinking? Did he feel like a general sending his troops into battle? Or was he just as scared as I was about it? There was nothing on his face to tell by.

The trucks were coming slowly on, 20 miles an hour. I wondered if they were going to plow right through the pack of pickets. But they didn't. When the first of them was about 20 feet from the thick mob of strikers, it stopped. The goon on the running board scrambled up onto the hood and, standing there, shouted something at the pickets. His voice came faintly through the window, but not loud enough for us to make out the words.

"I've got to go down there," Steve said. He turned from the window.

"Steve," Uncle Mort shouted in a harsh voice. "You're not to go down there. I forbid it."

"I have to," he said. He started for the door. Uncle Mort grabbed him by the sleeve of his jacket, but Steve was too strong for him. He pulled loose, ran for the office door, slammed it open, and ran through. Uncle Mort chased after him, but at the door he stopped, for he knew he could never catch up to Steve. "Steve," he cried, "Come back, come back." His voice echoed in the empty reception room. I could hear Steve's footsteps clatter on the stairs and then they faded away.

We all turned to the window again. The goon on the hood of the truck was still shouting at the pickets, his words floating up faintly. Behind him, the heads of the scabs were poked out around the canvas truck tops. One of the heads belonged to Charlie Henrich. Suddenly I remembered that day, so long ago, when Charlie had popped out of the alley beside Santini's grocery store, a 12-year-old kid wearing split shoes and a raggedy sweater. The strangest feeling came over me, and for a minute I wasn't sure where I was, here or back there. I felt pale and sweaty and I grabbed onto the window sill. Dad glanced at me. "Are you okay, Petey?"

"I'm okay," I said.

The goons were now clambering down from the trucks and trotting forward to form a loose line facing the pickets. Then Steve came into sight in the corner of the window, like a man running onto a picture. His yellow hair was flying, the sling flapping as he ran. Steve charged up to the goon on the truck hood who was doing the talking. They began to argue, their voices coming up to us like the distant barking of dogs. Now three or four of the goons surrounded Steve. One of them had his belly up against Steve's, and they stood there belly to belly, Steve and his yellow hair a half a head taller than the beefy, chunky man in the blue windbreaker.

Then something flew out of the crowd of pickets. It smacked against the windshield of the first truck with a cracking sound. The windshield shattered. Something else flew through the air, and another. Suddenly the pack of pickets broke. There was a swirling, the flashing of baseball bats, loud shouts and cries, a whirl of men in

wild confusion. Then there came three sharp cracks of
pistol fire, and suddenly everybody was flying in all
directions away from the factory gate. In seconds the
space in front of the gate was empty. Or almost empty:
for lying face down on the cold cement was a long body,
one leg crooked under the other, both hands down by his
sides, the sling laying loose on the ground. Spreading out
around the yellow hair was a splotch of red. It kept
growing like a flower bursting into bloom.

Epilogue

WHAT HAPPENED AFTERWARDS

In truth, Franklin D. Roosevelt's New Deal was not able to end the Depression. It went on into 1940. By that time World War II had started in Europe, and American industry was beginning to pick up as we began to supply weapons to England and Russia in their fight against Fascist Germany and Italy.

Then, in December 1941, the Japanese attacked the American naval base at Pearl Harbor, and the United States was now at war. The Federal government began to borrow huge sums of money to finance the war. Factories went into high gear, there were suddenly plenty of jobs for everybody, and the Depression was over.

Historians today still argue over the causes of the Depression of the 1930s, the worst in U.S. history. However, many agree that one serious problem was that by 1929, when the stock market crashed, too many American workers were being underpaid by comparison with people at the top. The net effect was that many ordinary workers could not afford to buy the very things they were making—all those automobiles, refrigerators, toasters, and so much else that American industry could turn out in large amounts. A lot of goods went unsold and piled up in warehouses. Factories began laying off workers, worsening the problem, and the downward spiral began.

Thereafter, nothing the government did could reverse the spiral. Not until the war forced the government to spend huge sums of borrowed money on war supplies was the spiral turned upwards.

Nevertheless, even though the New Deal did not end the Depression, it had profound effects on the United States and how we live today. In any earlier time, most Americans lived on farms that were pretty well self-sufficient. Farm families had to buy a few things, like ax heads, saddles, pins, and needles. But they made at home nearly everything else they needed. They had little need for a complex network of roads, of garbage collectors, of fire and police departments. Governments, both state and Federal, were small and touched people's lives very little.

But in the later years of the 19th century, there grew up in America (and elsewhere), the huge industrial system, based on cities, that is central to our lives today. More and more people looked to government to do important jobs, like regulating traffic, building roads, bridges, canals, running schools, subway systems and much more.

Still, before the Depression there remained a strong belief in America that the less governments got involved with things, the better: the least government was the best, it was said. In especial, many people believed that things would work out best for the nation as a whole if the free enterprise system was allowed to run unfettered by government controls.

The Depression changed Americans' thinking. It seemed clear that simply leaving business alone to run itself was not working. Americans no longer wanted a hands-off government but demanded that Congress, the President, governors, and mayors step in to solve the nation's problems. The New Deal began immediately to put in place a whole raft of new laws, orders, and acts that touched on virtually every aspect of American life.

Out of this mountain of new law, two pieces of legislation stand out. One was a series of acts, culminating in the Wagner Act of 1935, named for Senator Robert Wagner of New York. Their effect was to force business to negotiate with unions over matters like wages, hours, work conditions, and eventually, fringe benefits like vacations, pension plans, and medical plans.

Although it took years of struggle, in time American workers got a larger share of the prosperity they were instrumental in creating than they had before. They were now able to buy the things they were making—all those cars and toasters. Although we have had some economic downturns over the past half-century, none has been nearly as bad as the Great Depression. And despite occasional recessions, America has provided the greatest prosperity any society has ever given to ordinary people. It may be that we are too concerned with material things at the expense of other aspects of life, like family, friends, community; but it is nonetheless true that Americans are wealthy beyond the dreams of most of humanity elsewhere. And there is no doubt that the good wages most workers were eventually able to earn, in part because of New Deal legislation, played an important role in creating this prosperity.

The second crucially important innovation of the New Deal was Social Security. We take this program so much for granted today that we forget that when Petey Williamson was growing up there was no such thing—no welfare, no unemployment insurance, no government retirement payments, no government medical plans. If you lost your job, you had no money—none, and like the Williamsons would be dependent on relatives for food and shelter. Further, few companies provided pensions, medical plans, even paid vacations for most ordinary workers. Nor were working people usually able to save anything for old age. When they grew too old to work, they usually had to move in with their children whether they—or the children—liked it or not.

Today, of course, Social Security and related programs like Medicare provide all sorts of benefits, including pensions, unemployment payments, medical help, and much more. Roosevelt pushed hard to get Social Security passed, and he considered it one of his greatest achievements, which it undoubtedly was.

However, perhaps the most important innovation to come out of the New Deal government of the Depression was no specific act but an idea—the idea that government had a responsibility to help people in trouble, to do certain kinds of jobs that private enterprise won't or can't do, and to keep the economy running on an even keel.

We look to the Federal Reserve Board to set interest rates in order to keep the economy out of boom and bust cycles. We expect government to send us checks when we are out of work, to provide medical care for people who have no medical plans, and to help support the blind, the handicapped, and the elderly. We look to governments to run schools, fight wars, control air traffic, test our medicines for safety, and much, much more.

Some people believe that government is doing too much. There are even people who believe that programs like Social Security and the postal service ought to be turned over to private businesses. But in truth, when something goes wrong, either with us personally, or the country as a whole, we start asking the government to do something about it. For most Americans, it is not a question of "government interference," but of how much, and what, governments ought to do. For example, most Americans believe that government has a responsibility to check new drugs to make sure they are safe. Most Americans believe that government ought to audit banks from time to time to see that they are taking proper care of people's money. Most Americans believe that government ought to require manufacturers to follow certain health and safety rules. And in recent years, more and more Americans have come to believe that governments ought to pass laws to limit air and water pollution and otherwise improve our environment.

However, Americans are not all in agreement about how these, and other government practices, ought to be carried out. It is a question worth studying and arguing thoughtfully, for how it is decided affects all our lives.

How, then, did the New Deal affect Petey Williamson and his family? Writers, in truth, do not know any more about what happens to their characters after the story ends than readers do. However, we can make certain guesses. Petey Williamson was just the right age to have joined the army to fight in World War II. He probably would have gone to Officers Training School, and eventually, although not necessarily, have gone into combat. Hundreds of thousands of Americans were killed or wounded in the war, but the vast majority of service men and women survived, and we can assume that Petey did too. With the close of the war the government instituted the G.I. Bill of Rights, which among other things helped to pay for ex-soldiers' college educations. Petey would most likely have gone to college.

But in fact, it is probable that Victor Williamson could have paid for Petey's college education. The wartime economy benefited most Americans (except those who were in the military service), but it benefited manufacturers most. By the end of 1941, and perhaps earlier, Victor Williamson would have found a good job in a company making war goods. By the end of the war he would have risen in one company or another and would have been making a very good salary. In the prosperity that swept across America in the 1950s and 1960s he would almost certainly have done well for himself; and when he retired in the early 1960s, perhaps to the farm where he had grown up, he would have lived on his Social Security checks and a good pension.

Charlie Henrich, too, would almost certainly have served in the military during the war. Indeed, he might have joined the army right at the beginning, when it was expanding to meet the threat of war in Europe. After the war he might well have taken advantage of the G.I. Bill to go to college and thereafter, carved out a career for himself, although he would certainly have never forgotten the experience of living in Shacktown for several years.

Ruth Williamson, too, might have taken advantage of wartime prosperity to go back to college, but by that time she would have been in her mid-20s. She might have married, but during the war a lot of jobs in factories and elsewhere opened up for women because so many men were away on military service. Perhaps she, too, found a career for herself.

How would Petey Williamson have lived his life? We can only guess. His father and his uncle were both businessmen, so he might have been drawn into business. But it is more likely that the events told in this book would have made him something of a social critic—as the Depression did to many young people who endured it. Perhaps he became a journalist covering Washington, perhaps a labor lawyer working with unions. We cannot be sure.

But he certainly would never have forgotten that the good things that came with post-war prosperity were paid for by people who fought, and sometimes died, in the battles of the Depression.